AF443284

Ecological Risk Assessment Decision-Support System: A Conceptual Design

Recent titles from the
Society of Environmental Toxicology and
Chemistry (SETAC)

Principles and Processes for Evaluating Endocrine Disruption in Wildlife
Kendall, Dickerson, Giesy, Suk, editors
1998

Quantitative-Structure Activity Relationships in Environmental Science-VII
Chen and Schüürmann, editors
1997

Atmospheric Deposition of Contaminants to the Great Lakes and Coastal Waters
Baker, editor
1997

Chemically Induced Alterations in Functional Development and Reproduction of Fishes
Rolland, Gilbertson, Peterson, editors
1997

Chemical Ranking and Scoring: Guidelines for Relative Assessment of Chemicals
Swanson and Socha, editors
1997

Ecological Risk Assessment of Contaminated Sediments
Ingersoll, Dillon, Biddinger, editors
1997

Public Policy Applications of Life-cycle Assessment
Allen, Consoli, Davis, Fava, Warren, editors
1997

Reassessment of Metals Criteria for Aquatic Life Protection: Priorities for Research and Implementation
Bergman and Dorward-King, editors
1997

Multi-media Fate Model: A Vital Tool for Predicting the Fate of Chemicals
Cowan, Mackay, Feijtel, van de Meent, Di Guardo, Davies, Mackay, editors
1995

For information about additional titles or about SETAC's international journal,
Environmental Toxicology and Chemistry,
contact the SETAC Office, 1010 N. 12th Avenue, Pensacola, FL USA 32501-3370
T 850 469 1500   F 850 469 9778   E setac@setac.org   http://www.setac.org

Ecological Risk Assessment Decision-Support System: A Conceptual Design

Edited by

Kevin H. Reinert
Rohm and Haas Company

Steven M. Bartell
SENES Oak Ridge, Inc.

Gregory R. Biddinger
Exxon Company, U.S.A.

Proceedings of the Pellston Workshop on Ecological Risk Assessment Modeling
23–28 August 1994
Pellston, Michigan

SETAC Special Publications Series

SETAC Liaison
Greg Schiefer
Society of Environmental Toxicology and Chemistry (SETAC)

Current Coordinating Editor of SETAC Books
Christopher G. Ingersoll
U.S. Geological Survey, Midwest Science Center

Publication sponsored by the Society of Environmental Toxicology and Chemistry (SETAC) and the SETAC Foundation for Environmental Education

Cover design by Mike Kinney
Indexing by IRIS

Library of Congress Cataloging-in-Publication Data

SETAC Ecological Risk Assessment Modeling Workshop (1994 : Pellston. Mich.)
Ecological risk assessment decision-support system : a conceptual design/edited by Kevin H. Reinert, Steven M. Bartell, Gregory R. Biddinger.
p. cm.
"SETAC Ecological Risk Assessment Modeling Workshop, August 23–28, 1995, Pellston, Michigan."
Includes bibliographical references.
ISBN 1-880611-11-2 (hc)
I. Ecological risk assessment—Congresses. 2. Decision-support systems-Congresses. I. Reinert, Kevin H. (Kevin Howard), 1956–. II. Bartell, Seven M. III. Biddinger, Gregory R. IV. SETAC (Society) V. Title.
QH541.15.R57S48 1994
363.1'02—DC21   98-36346
                                                                                                          CIP

Information in this book was obtained from individual experts and highly regarded sources. It is the publisher's intent to print accurate and reliable information, and numerous references are cited; however, the authors, editors, and publisher cannot be responsible for the validity of all information presented here or for the consequences of its use. Information contained herein does not necessarily reflect the policy or views of the Society of Environmental Toxicology and Chemistry (SETAC) or the SETAC Foundation for Environmental Education.

International Standard Book Number 1-880611-11-2
Printed in the United States of America
05 04 03 02 01 00 99 98   10 9 8 7 6 5 4 3 2 1

♾The paper used in this publication meets the minimum requirements of the American National Standard for Information Sciences—Permanence of Paper for Printed Library Materials, ANSI Z39.48-1984.

Reference listing: Reinert KH, Bartell SM, Biddinger GR, editors. 1998. Ecological risk assessment decision-support system: a conceptual design. Proceedings from SETAC Ecological Risk Assessment Modeling Workshop; 1994 Aug 23–28; Pellston MI. Pensacola FL: Society of Environmental Toxicology and Chemistry. 120 p.

The SETAC Special Publications Series

The SETAC Special Publications Series was established by the Society of Environmental Toxicology and Chemistry (SETAC) to provide in-depth reviews and critical appraisals on scientific subjects relevant to understanding the impact of chemicals and technology on the environment. The series consists of single- and multiple-authored or edited books on topics reviewed and recommended by the SETAC Board of Directors for their importance, timeliness, and contribution to multidisciplinary approaches to solving environmental problems. The diversity and breadth of subjects covered in the series reflect the wide range of disciplines encompassed by environmental toxicology, environmental chemistry, and hazard and risk assessment. Despite this diversity, the goals of these volumes are similar; they are to present the reader with authoritative coverage of the literature, as well as paradigms, methodologies and controversies, research needs, and new developments specific to the featured topics. All books in the series are peer reviewed for SETAC by acknowledged experts.

The SETAC Special Publications are useful to environmental scientists in research, research management, chemical manufacturing, regulation, and education, as well as to students considering careers in these areas. The series provides information for keeping abreast of recent developments in familiar subject areas and for rapid introduction to principles and approaches in new subject areas.

SETAC would like to recognize the past SETAC Special Publications Series editors:

T.W. La Point
   The Institute for Environmental and Human Health
   Texas Tech University
   Lubbock, TX

B.T. Walton
   U.S. Environmental Protection Agency
   Research Triangle Park, NC

C.H. Ward
   Department of Environmental Sciences and Engineering
   Rice University
   Houston, TX

Contents

Chapter 1
Introduction 1
K. Reinert and S. Bartell

Chapter 2
Problem formulation 7
C. van Leeuwen, G. Biddinger, D. Gess, D. Moore, T. Natan, D. Winkelmann

Chapter 3
Model selection considerations in fate-and-effects analysis 15
B. Parkhurst, S. Christensen, R. Goldstein, B. Neely, and K. Solomon

Chapter 4
Risk characterization 21
J. Lipton, D. Cacela, C. Cowan, P. deFur, L. Ginzburg, and C. Mebane

Chapter 5
Obtaining data for ecological risk assessment 29
S. Bradbury, J. Hermens, W. Karcher, G. Niemi, R. Purdy, and C. Richards

Chapter 6
Model testing and evaluation.....................................39
A. Venkatram, L. Burns, C. Chen, J. Irwin, and M. Johnson

List of figures

List of tables

Foreword

International experts in software, hardware, ecological modeling, model user groups, risk assessment, and risk management met to participate in a workshop to discuss and design an ecological risk assessment decision-support system (ERADSS). The workshop process was split into 3 main sections: 1) case study role-playing simulations, 2) discussion of system components (e.g., problem formulation, risk characterization, etc.), and 3) a system-design group. Initially, pairs of risk manager/assessor teams presented separate case studies in succession. The remainder of the conference attendees worked with their respective component groups and completed an ecological risk assessment (ERA) for each case study. The system-design group was centrally located during the role playing so that the members could visually observe the interactions between the component groups and the risk manager/assessor teams. The paired risk manager/assessor team kept the assessment on track and presented their learnings, both positive and negative, to the conference. The system-design group later presented its observations and potential methods for design of a working decision-support system.

Next, the model system component groups discussed the strengths and weaknesses observed in each of the case studies from the perspective of their respective component. State-of-the-art methods for each component in the context of the modeling system, how well the component could fit into the system, evident data gaps, fixes for the data gaps, and next steps toward implementation were also addressed. During this period, the system-design group continued to refine the potential model system based on oral reports from the previous day's and evening's discussions.

After reports from the component groups and the system-design group, all participants were reshuffled into 3 replicate groups to concurrently discuss system needs, unresolved technical issues, and other issues concerning the use of the current version of the decision-support system. Each case study group consisted of members from each component group, including 1 member from the system-design group. Concurrently, the system-design group and several members from the steering committee (framework group) continued to refine the modeling system, while considering potential users and uses of the system.

The next plenary session dealt with reports from the case studies and presentation of the revised modeling system. Discussion centered around potential system linkages and system needs. The final plenary session discussed whether expectations were met, next steps in the design of the system, and a potential implementation scheme.

The commitment of the workshop participants to advancing ecological risk assessment and the underlying science is appreciated.

Sincere thanks is also expressed to the authors who gave many hours of their time to generate this document. Special recognition is also given to Linda Burg (Rohm and Haas Company), Linda Longsworth (SETAC), and Cheri Mertins (SETAC) who labored to make the workshop a reality and this publication a success.

The editors acknowledge the excellent editorial support of Chris Englert and Stacey Hagman at SETAC and the helpful technical suggestions of Dave Mauriello at USEPA who critically reviewed the proceedings.

Preface

This book presents the proceedings of the 19th Pellston Workshop held in Pellston, Michigan from 23–28 August 1994 at the University of Michigan Biological Station, the site of many workshops since the Pellston series began in 1977. Similar to other workshops in this series, expert participation was invited from government, academia, public interest groups, and industry. Invited participants were selected based on their demonstrated interest and experience concerning ecological risk assessment, development of decision-support systems, or both. The workshop provided an organized format for exchanging ideas, debate, and development of consensus concerning the many unresolved issues associated with the application of ecological risk assessment and the conceptual design of a decision-support system. These proceedings reflect the state-of-the-art at the time of the workshop and focus on the components of ecological risk assessment and on their possible integration into a conceptual design for a decision-support system. Potential approaches toward realizing this vision were explored at the workshop and are outlined in this volume.

Acknowledgments

The workshop and this publication were made possible by financial support from the following organizations:

American Forest and Paper Association

American Industrial Health Council

Chemical Manufacturers Association

DNV Technica Ltd.

Electric Power Research Institute

Environment Canada

Exxon Corporation

National Council of the Paper Industry for Air and Stream Improvement

Rohm and Haas Company

U.S. Environmental Protection Agency

Editors

Kevin H. Reinert is the Research Section Manager of the Ecotoxicology and Ecological Risk Assessment Section in the Toxicology Department of the Rohm and Haas Company, Spring House, Pennsylvania. Dr. Reinert received his M.S. in environmental sciences from Rutgers University (1981) and earned a Ph.D. in biological sciences at the University of North Texas in 1984. He has worked as a Physical Scientist with the U.S. Army Corps of Engineers, a Senior Ecotoxicologist at 3M, and Manager of Risk Services at SMC Environmental Services group, an environmental consulting firm. In his current position, Dr. Reinert manages the section responsible for the conduct of corporate environmental toxicology and fate studies, environmental fate and transport modeling, and ecological risk assessment. He is responsible for numerous publications and presentations in the areas described above. Dr. Reinert is active in numerous industry trade groups, and he has participated in AIBS NASA Scientific Review Panels and USEPA Risk Assessment Forum peer review. He currently serves as an OECD Test Guideline Reviewer. He is a member of the Pennsylvania Cleanup Standards Science Advisory Board (chairs Risk Assessment Subcommittee). Dr. Reinert serves on the editorial board of the journal, *Human and Ecological Risk Assessment.* He has been listed in several Who's Who publications and has attended several recent SETAC Pellston Conferences.

Dr. Reinert has been active in SETAC since 1981, and he received the SETAC/Procter & Gamble Doctoral Fellowship Award in 1984. Dr. Reinert spent 6 years on the *ET&C* Editorial Board, chaired sessions at 4 recent SETAC annual meetings, and chaired the Ecological Risk Assessment Symposium at the 14th Annual Meeting in Houston. Dr. Reinert was a member of the ad hoc Scientific Initiatives and the Long-Range Planning Committees. He currently serves on the ad hoc Committee on Chemist Involvement in SETAC and the SETAC Technical Committee, and he was President of the Hudson-Delaware Regional Chapter from 1994–1995.

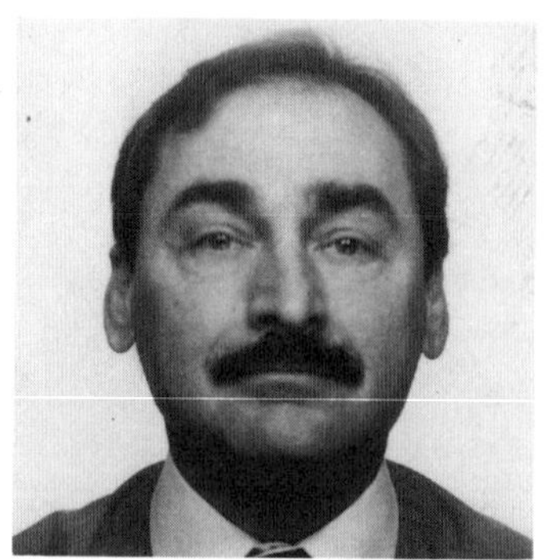

Steven M. Bartell is Vice President and Director of SENES Oak Ridge, Inc., Center for Risk Analysis in Oak Ridge, Tennessee. He also holds an adjunct faculty appointment in the Department of Ecology and Evolutionary Biology at the University of Tennessee, Knoxville. Dr. Bartell received an M.S. in botany (1973) and earned his Ph.D. in limnology and oceanography (1978), both from the University of Wisconsin, Madison. Dr. Bartell's professional training focused on quantitative ecology, systems analysis, and numerical modeling. He worked as a senior scientist at the Savannah River Ecology Laboratory (1978-80), where he developed an environmental transport model for polynuclear aromatic hydrocarbons for streams and rivers. In 1980, he joined the Aquatic Ecology Section in the Environmental Sciences Division at Oak Ridge National Laboratory and served as a research associate, research staff member, and group leader until 1992. His primary research activities included environmental transport modeling, theoretical systems ecology, development and evaluation of bioenergetics models of populations and ecosystems, ecological risk assessment, and global climate change. In 1992, Dr. Bartell became a principal at SENES Oak Ridge, Inc., where he now manages and is responsible for the corporation's activities in ecological risk assessment and sustainable resource development. Dr. Bartell has been involved nationally and internationally in the development of frameworks and approaches for assessing ecological risks. He has authored numerous book chapters, technical articles, and other publications concerning topics in theoretical and applied ecology. He is the principal author of *Ecological Risk Estimation*, Lewis Publishers (1992), and is co-author and contributor to the ecological risk section to *Risk Assessment and Management Handbook for Environmental, Health and Safety Professionals*, McGraw-Hill (1996).

Dr. Bartell is a member of the Environmental Process and Effects Committee of the USEPA's Science Advisory Board. He also serves on the editorial boards of *Human and Ecological Risk Assessment* and *Chemosphere* and is a past member of the editorial board of *Ecological Applications*. He has been a long-time member of SETAC and has assisted in the review of SETAC publications.

Gregory R. Biddinger is presently an Advisor for Exxon Company, USA, in the Environmental and Safety Department. He obtained his doctoral training in Aquatic Ecology and Physiology at Indiana State University and subsequently trained in environmental toxicology while a post-doctoral associate at Cornell University. Since 1983, Dr. Biddinger has worked as an environmental toxicologist for the Illinois Environmental Protection Agency and Exxon, developing and directing programs to manage the risks of chemicals in the marketplace and the safe disposal of wastes from manufacturing processes. During the time of this workshop, Dr. Biddinger was in charge of the Environmental Toxicology Section for Exxon and Biomedical Sciences, Inc., located in East Millstone, NJ.

During his career, Dr. Biddinger has been actively involved in the advancement and standardization of testing methods in environmental toxicology and risk assessment. Since 1992 he has held the position of Chair for SETAC's Ecological Risk Assessment Advisory Group.

Executive summary

The 19th Pellston workshop was held in Pellston, Michigan on 23–28 Aug 1994 to explore the feasibility, efficacy, and potential design of an ecological risk assessment decision-support system (ERADSS) for use by risk assessors and risk managers. Participants were involved in the following aspects of the system design during this workshop:

- identification of state-of-the-art approaches and models in each subdiscipline or component (e.g., fate analysis), including data needs;
- definition of system structure hardware and rules for operation;
- development of file management, model management and data management components;
- description of gateways for entry into the modeling system and data selection and manipulation;
- integration of the ability to build and test new and reworked models within the system;
- standardization of future model development; and
- development of a general plan for completion, including priorities, potential development time, and costs.

The development of expert systems for ecological risk assessment (ERA) was identified during a Society of Environmental Toxicology and Chemistry (SETAC) workshop held in Breckenridge, Colorado in 1987 to help make databases and complex loading, exposure, and effects models accessible and efficient for users. The need for the system was identified over 5 years ago and was finally addressed in detail during this workshop.

A collaborative effort to address ERA using modeling systems is needed. Such joint efforts would diminish redundancy and overlap, reduce the inconsistency and compatibilities that currently exist among these approaches and modeling systems, and could result in numerous benefits associated with consensus on use of the best tools regardless of national boundaries.

Background

The assessment of ecological risk is a rapidly evolving discipline that is quickly being incorporated into the daily routines of industry and government to measure ecological risks arising from a product's life cycle. Ecological risk assessment is being applied to the assessment of new and existing chemicals and products, process releases, and waste sites to assess the potential for damage due to the current or future presence of chemical contaminants and other types of stressors.

Ecological risk assessment frameworks have recently been completed or are under development in numerous countries such as the United States, Canada, and Europe (e.g.,

xvi

Germany, The Netherlands, United Kingdom). Coordination of these initiatives, activities, and their supporting research programs has not been formalized. Methods are often incompatible due to the numerous approaches and models developed for specific, often narrow, needs or end uses. Consequently, models exist in numerous subdisciplines of ERA, such as chemical property-and-fate estimation, toxicity, biological uptake, and population effects. Because of limited coordination across these subdisciplines and a lack of clarity on the types of questions that need to be addressed, these models may not be adequately developed or used appropriately within the discipline of ERA.

Benefits of an ERADSS

We expect the following specific benefits from the design and implementation of an ERADSS:

- creation of an informal or formal international information transfer network;
- provision of an "audit trail" for assessments;
- creation of various concepts and designs, leading eventually to a tool to advance the institutionalization of ERA into risk management;
- greater confidence in results from the assessments;
- identification and quantification of assessment uncertainties;
- fostering of global harmonization of ERA and development of common methods, data and criteria;
- development of minimum criteria for model design and promotion of model compatibility; and
- pooled resources to obtain more cost-effective, consistent, and flexible systems with reduced duplication of effort and incompatibilities.

Risk-assessment process evaluation and system design

Ecological risk assessment is one key part of the process of environmental risk management. This process involves 3 major groups of participants, each of whom can also be considered end-users of the decision-support system:

- affected or interested parties,
- risk managers, and
- risk assessors.

Each group has a specific role in this process. The development of a decision-support system for ERA depends upon an understanding of the underlying process used by these groups. This system can either address routine assessments (e.g., new chemical notification) or explore novel assessments to hypothetical problems. The assessment process typically starts and ends with stakeholders or interested parties who may be from public agencies, industry, private firms, special interest groups, or other organizations. They are responsible for identifying a potential environmental problem and for determining whether it has been resolved. In this process, they interact primarily with risk managers. Risk managers, in turn, are responsible for formulating the environmental problem with risk assessors and for developing recommendations based on both technical and value considerations. They interact with both stakeholders and risk assessors. Risk assessors are responsible for the technical evaluation of ecological risk and interact primarily with risk managers.

Workshop conclusions and products

The workshop produced several alternative designs for a decision-support system for ERA. A larger, comprehensive system would provide information, data, model access and integration, and computational capabilities for performing risk assessments in a probabilistic framework that is linked functionally to a decision-support system for risk assessment. An alternative system which could likely be more easily assembled was proposed. The data and model identification and acquisition (DMIA) system, would identify data, models, and other tools that could contribute to assessing ecological risks in individual applications and facilitate access through the Internet. Of all the approaches identified at the workshop, development of the DMIA appears to merit primary attention as a prototype system. Although this system initially would not operationally integrate data, models, and other tools to perform the assessment, it could evolve into a more complete assessment-support system.

The products from this workshop include an executive summary, this report, and a workplan that was subsequently developed and presented at meetings such as ASTM Ecological Risk Assessment, SETAC, and CEFIC, Organization for Economic Cooperation and Development and to government agencies such as U.S. Environmental Protection Agency, Environment Canada, and various European agencies. After presentation and incorporation of feedback, a peer-reviewed planning document under the auspices of the SETAC Foundation for Environmental Education could be prepared. This document will then be used to begin the development of the ERADSS. The SETAC Foundation for Environmental Education is recommended as a neutral platform for coordinating funds and managing the prototype development.

Implementation strategy/next steps

Key steps in the development process of a decision-support system for ERA include:

- production of a scoping document for use in peer review, user focus surveys, and discussions with potential funding sources;
- establishment of a Steering group under the SETAC Ecological Risk Assessment Advisory Group to explore approaches to funding, managing, maintaining, and updating a decision-support system;
- definition of the scope of the prototype system; and
- implementation and enhancement of the prototype system.

Based on the current trends in computing and the state at which models continue to evolve, development of the DMIA concept appears to be a more fruitful first step.

Abbreviations

AI	artificial intelligence
ASTM	American Society for Testing and Materials
BACI	before-after control-impact
CI	confidence interval
CAA	Clean Air Act
CBA	cost-benefit analysis
CEFIC	European Chemical Industry Council
CERCLA	Comprehensive Environmental Response, Compensation and Liability Act
CESARS	Chemical Evaluation and Retrieval System
CIESIN	Consortium of International Earth Science Information Networks
CLOGP	computerized log of the octanol-water partition coefficient
CWA	Clean Water Act
DAL	data access language
DBA	dependency bounds analysis
DBMS	database management system
DMIA	data and model identification and acquisition
DOE	Department of Energy
DSS	decision-support system
EEC	expected environmental concentration
EPRI	Electric Power Research Institute
ERA	ecological risk assessment
ERADSS	ecological risk assessment decision-support system
EU	European Union
FIFRA	U.S. Federal Insecticide, Fungicide and Rodenticide Act
FTP	file transfer protocol

GIS	Geographic Information System
HTML	Hyper Text Markup Language
IUCLID	International Unified Chemicals Information Database
IRIS	integrated risk information system
JRC	Joint Research Commission
LCA	life-cycle assessment
NEPA	National Environmental Protection Act
NOEC	no observed effect concentration
NTIS	National Technical Information Service
OECD	Organization for Economic Cooperation and Development
OPA	USEPA Office of Policy Analysis
PAH	polycyclic aromatic hydrocarbon
pK_a	acid dissociation constant
QA	quality assurance
QC	quality control
QSAR	quantitative structure-activity relationship
RA	risk assessment
RCRA	Resource Conservation and Recovery Act
RM	risk manager
SAS	Statistical Analysis System
SEDSS	Sandia Environmental Decision-Support System
SETAC	Society of Environmental Toxicology and Chemistry
SQL	structured query language
STORET	Storage and Retrieval Data System
TCA	trichloroethane
TCDF	tetprachlorodibenzofuran
TSCA	Toxic Substances Control Act
URL	uniform resource locator
USGS	United States Geological Survey

| WAIS | wide area information servers |
| WWW | world wide web |

SETAC Press

Chapter 1

Introduction

K. Reinert and S. Bartell

Ecological risk assessment (ERA) is a continually evolving discipline that is becoming increasingly important in the environmental affairs of government and industry. Some major areas of current and future applications of ERA include site remediation, assessment of off-site ecological impacts, evaluation of process wastes, facility location, landscape planning, and product development.

Methods for assessing ecological risks are being developed in the United States (U.S. Environmental Protection Agency [USEPA]), Canada, various European countries, the European Union, and elsewhere. The methods share many components and processes (e.g., chemical toxicity profiles, chemical fate-and-effects models, bioaccumulation, considerations of uncertainty, etc.). However, the coordination of these activities among countries has not been a priority. The resulting methodologies are often incompatible, in part because they have been designed to meet different needs. The current state of ERA might be summarized as follows: 1) data needs are different, depending on the regulatory framework, 2) numerous models and methods exist that could be coordinated in an integrated ERA system, 3) the currently available methods are not integrated, thus making ERA potentially inconsistent and inefficient, and 4) identical ecological threats can result in different assessments of ecological risks, simply as a result of different assessment methods.

A clear need exists to stimulate a collaborative effort to address method development for ERA and the design of an ecological risk assessment decision-support system (ERADSS). The workshop steering committee intentionally designed the workshop to parallel USEPA's Framework for Ecological Risk Assessment (USEPA 1992) shown in Figure 1-1.

19th SETAC Pellston Workshop

The 19th SETAC Pellston Workshop was organized to address the feasibility of designing and developing an automated decision-support system for assessing ecological risks. The subject of the workshop has historical precedence within SETAC. Participants attending the 1987 SETAC workshop at Breckenridge, Colorado, recognized the need for an expert system for ERA and recommended the development of this system (Fava et al. 1987).

Such a system would not only increase the accessibility of complex exposure-and-effects models, but also would facilitate exposure and effects and risk analysis and would expedite ERA.

The steering committee organized this workshop to consider the development of a decision-support system for performing ERA. The result of this effort was the August 1994 Pellston Workshop, where invited participants addressed the following aspects of system design:

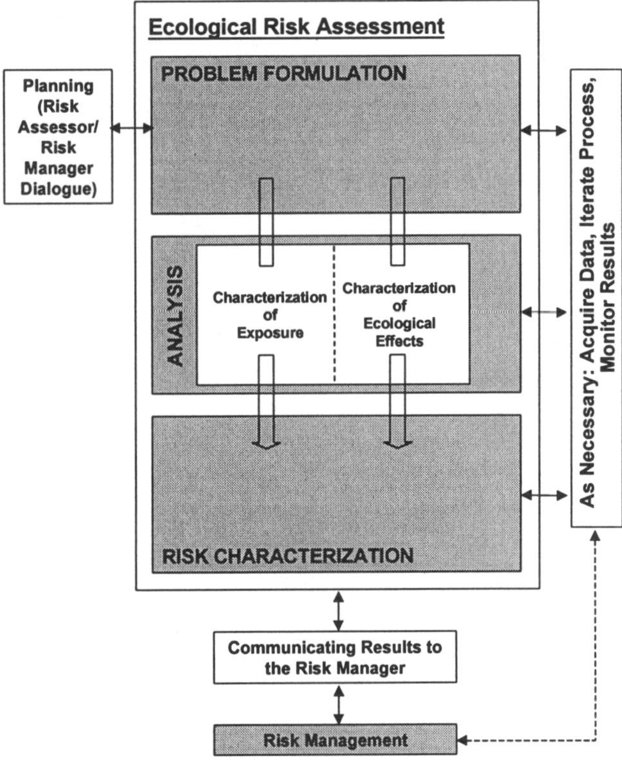

Figure 1-1   USEPA framework for ecological risk assessment

- identification of state-of-the-art methods and models within each of the component disciplines (i.e., problem formulation, risk characterization) required for ERA,
- definition of decision-support system structure and its operation,
- development of data and model management,
- description of user entry into model and data selection,
- capability to develop and integrate new or modified models within the system,
- standardization of model development for use in ERA, and
- development of a general plan for system development, including priorities, time, and potential cost.

Several benefits were anticipated as the result of the development of a decision-support system for ERA:

- creation of a network for international information transfer,
- creation of concepts and design, leading eventually to a tool to advance the standardization of ERA,
- fostering global harmonization of ERA approaches,
- development of a set of minimal criteria for model implementation, and

- reducing the cost of tool development through the pooling of resources from different groups.

The workshop process

Internationally recognized experts in ERA, ecological modeling, data analysis, expert systems technology, and potential users participated in the week-long workshop (Figure 1-2). The workshop began by using the participants in their respective technical roles to simulate a decision-support system for ERA. In an ERA "theater," risk manager/risk assessor teams used this system to address ecological risks posed in 3 hypothetical case studies.

These case studies were as follows:

- use of 1,1,1–trichloroethane in Canada,
- Commencement Bay Superfund site in Washington, USA, and
- spotted owl habitat protection in northwestern USA.

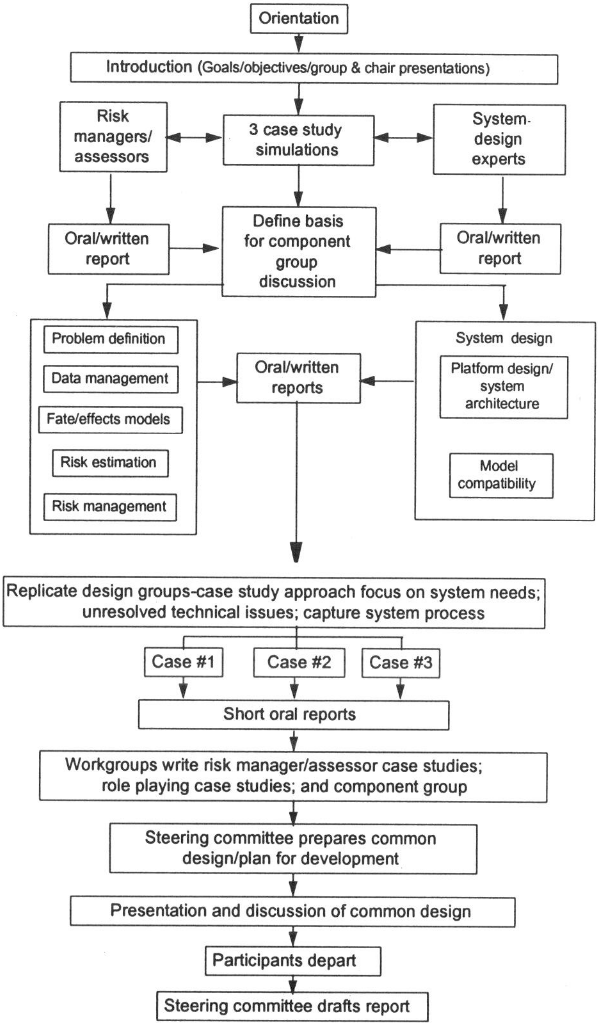

Figure 1-2 Ecological risk assessment modeling workshop

The invited professionals in expert systems technology observed the "theater" to 1) learn more about the nature and process of ERA and 2) formulate an initial impression concerning the feasibility of automating the ERA process. Following the case history risk-assessment theater, all participants reviewed what had occurred, how the managers and assessors used the system, as well as how the system (i.e., the experts) responded, and the important interactions among the system components in each of the case studies.

The second activity of the workshop organized the participants into discussion groups according to their area of technical expertise (e.g., modelers, data analysts, ecotoxicologists, etc.). The objective of these discussions was to determine the current strengths and feasibility of each ERA component towards the development of an ERADSS. Current limitations and future needs specific to each discipline were also addressed in these groups. At the same time, the system design group refined its earlier concept of a prototype ERADSS. Representatives of each of the technical specialty groups and the system-design group orally presented the results of the group deliberations.

Workshop participants were then assigned to 1 of 3 replicate groups, each charged with the purpose of designing a decision-support system for ecological risk analysis and each focusing on applying their system to 1 of the 3 case studies. Each replicate group also had 1 member from the systems design team. During this time, members of the steering committee and the remaining system designers worked to refine the earlier ERADSS, considered potential users of the system, and speculated on the actual use of the ERADSS. The reports from each of the replicate system design groups and the presentation of the revised ERADSS were discussed at the subsequent plenary session.

The final plenary session summarized the workshop, discussed the strengths and limitations of the proposed system, revisited the original expectations of the workshop, and discussed possible strategies and specific next steps for implementing the ERADSS. Throughout the workshop, written reports and summary documents were prepared and submitted to the steering committee. This information provided the raw material for the preparation of this book.

Chapter description

This book summarizes the 19th SETAC Pellston Workshop, which was organized to examine the need for and efficacy of a standardized modeling approach for assessing ecological risks. The volume consists of 8 chapters followed by appendixes that present the results of the workshop. Each chapter provides an overview of the discipline in relation to the design of an ERADSS. As appropriate, a statement outlining technical advances necessary to realize the desired decision-support system (DSS) is included.

Chapter 1 describes the Pellston Workshop process and briefly introduces the various case studies discussed during the workshop. Chapters 2 through 6 introduce the separate risk-assessment components and the technical disciplines that must be organized and integrated to produce the ERADSS. Chapter 2 considers the incorporation of the problem-formulation component of ERA into a decision-support system for ERA. Chapter 3 discusses model selection consideration for assessing the fate and effects of chemicals and other ecological stressors in the environment. Chapter 4 addresses the process of risk characterization in the context of the decision-support system. Chapter 5 focuses on the data needed for ERA and its incorporation into the support system. Chapter 6 summarizes approaches to model testing and evaluation required in the selection of models to be included in the ERADSS. Chapter 7 presents several possible designs for the ERADSS.

Chapter 8 outlines the steps for implementing the prototype of an ERADSS and discusses DSS development and possible implementation.

Case studies

The conference used case studies as a means of examining the processes used in ERA and for initially exploring the feasibility of an ERADSS. Three intentionally different cases were selected prior to the workshop. The case studies presented a range of differently scaled stressors and endpoints, including local, regional, and global concerns. Assessments of past as well as future stressors were included. These cases were developed primarily to examine the process of the risk assessments, not to perform the definitive assessments.

The case studies were visited twice: once on the first day by the entire group divided into teams (case history risk-assessment theater) and a second time on day 3 by subgroups. The first case study exercise divided the participants according to component risk-assessment technical specialties previously assigned by the steering committee. Manager/assessor teams for each case began the process and then managed the assessment process as different component groups considered questions and issues. The entire group examined all 3 case studies.

The second case study exercise involved 3 subgroups, each using a common pathway or decision system and 1 or more representatives from each of the component groups. Each subgroup conducted a single case study and reported back to the whole group at a subsequent meeting. The 3 case study exercises are reported in Appendix B.

Chapter 2

Problem formulation

C. van Leeuwen, G. Biddinger, D. Gess, D. Moore, T. Natan, D. Winkelmann

The purpose of the problem-formulation phase in an ecological risk assessment (ERA) is to establish the goals, breadth, and focus of the problem such that the results of the analyses will be useful to the risk manager charged with making an environmental decision. The end product of this phase is a conceptual model that relates the nature of the ecological disturbance to the ecological effects of concern (i.e., the assessment endpoints) (see Suter 1993), the data required to perform the assessment, and the analyses to be used (USEPA 1992).

At the Pellston workshop, the problem-formulation group was charged with defining the process a risk manager and risk assessor should follow to proceed from the initial problem confronting the risk manager (i.e., the environmental decision required) to the conceptual model that describes how the ERA will proceed. This systematic planning phase is crucial to reduce the potential of failing to adequately address the important issues as initially conceived by the risk manager, stakeholders, and the public. Interestingly, in working through all 3 case studies, manager/assessor teams encountered difficulty in defining a conceptual model that clearly described the nature of the stressors and the anticipated ecological impacts. It proved difficult to avoid jumping directly into discussions of data, models, and the analysis of risks.

The following sections describe the process of problem-formulation and then describe in more detail each of the steps in the process. The chapter ends with some speculation concerning how an expert or decision-support system would improve the problem-formulation phase of ERA.

2.1 Overview of problem formulation

The process begins with a risk manager confronted by a situation suggesting potential ecological risk and requiring a decision to avoid, reduce, or remediate that risk. To make an appropriate decision, the risk manager must consider and define the regulatory, technical, and socio-economic context of the problem (Figure 2-1). With this information, the risk manager and the risk assessor then need to define the goals of the assessment so that the eventual results can be used by the risk manager to make a decision. To do this, con-

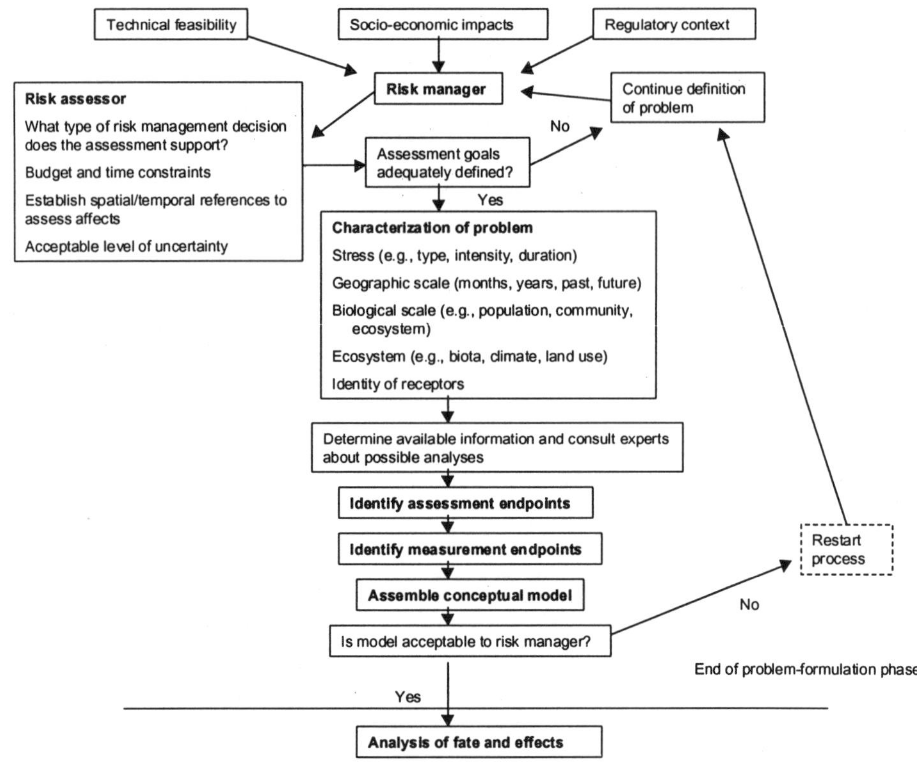

Figure 2-1   Flow diagram for problem-formulation phase

sideration must be given to the type of risk management decision required. For example, might the widespread application of a new pesticide produce unacceptable effects on nontarget passerine birds? Budget constraints, time limitations, spatial and temporal scales, selection of reference points, and uncertainty all enter into the assessment and influence the ability of the risk manager to make a reasonable and scientifically defensible environmental decision.

Once the risk manager and risk assessor have both agreed upon the goals of the ERA, the next step is for the risk assessor to further outline the technical aspects of the problem. This requires characterizing the stressors, geographic and temporal scales, biological levels of organization, ecosystems, and the receptors potentially exposed to the stressor. To assist in this characterization, the assessor should consult the literature, existing databases, and scientific experts to determine the available information and to help identify assessment endpoints and possible analytical approaches.

The information compiled during the exchange between the risk manager and risk assessor and from the consultations with scientific experts is then used to identify the assessment endpoints (Figure 2-1 and Moore and Biddinger 1995). Assessment endpoints are statements about the ecological values we wish to protect and are usually defined in terms of population, community, or ecosystem properties (e.g., risks of population extinction, reductions in species richness, or changes in system nutrient flows) (Suter 1993). Assessment endpoints might not be directly measurable (e.g., potential effects of a new substance on populations of peregrine falcons) and thus measurement endpoints (e.g., tissue levels causing mortality to falcon egg embryos) that are related to the assessment endpoints are used as an alternative (Barnthouse 1992). Measurement endpoints commonly include toxicity tests and field surveys. Once the assessment and measurement endpoints have been defined, the next step in the problem-formulation process is to prepare a conceptual model.

The conceptual model is a "series of working hypotheses regarding how the stressor might affect ecological components of the natural environment" (NRC 1986). The conceptual model also includes statements about the ecosystem under consideration and the relationship between measurement and assessment endpoints (USEPA 1992). As a final check to ensure that the ERA is proceeding in the right direction, the risk assessor should verify with the risk manager that the proposed conceptual model will provide the information needed to support the manager in making the environmental decision. Once agreement has been reached on the conceptual model, the assessment advances from the problem-formulation phase to the analysis phase.

2.2   The role of ecological risk assessment in risk management

Historically, the roles of the risk assessor and the risk manager have been separated (NRC 1986). However, to effectively design and execute an assessment, the risk assessor must understand the management context of the problem. If the selected risk assessment endpoints and ultimate expression of risk are not compatible with the needs of the manager, the risk assessment might not be useful, even if technically accurate. Therefore, a decision-support system for ERAs could provide a valuable contribution to problem formulation by enhancing the necessary dialogue between the risk assessor and the risk manager.

There are at least 3 principal areas in which risk management decisions are required: product safety, site management, and natural resource use. Selected examples from each of these 3 areas are presented in Table 2-1.

Risk management involves making decisions that explicitly consider the likelihood of adverse effects to the environment together with other factors, such as economic, social, technical, and legal issues (Figure 2-2). The decision-makers may be from business, government, or the general public. The drivers for risk assessment can be regulatory in nature or can be the result of outside pressures from various stakeholders. Risk managers usually must choose among alternative courses of action, generally in the face of significant levels of uncertainty.

Risk managers need to determine the criteria that will be used to compare and select from various alternatives. Depending on the specific decision, a risk manager may wish to consider the costs and risks for all activities in the full life cycle of each alternative. For example, a regulatory decision of whether to approve the use of a new chemical needs to

Table 2-1   Areas requiring risk management

Area	Type	Examples
Product environmental health and safety	New chemicals Existing chemicals Biotechnology	Pre-manufacturing notices Pesticide re-evaluations Permits to release genetically modified organisms
Site management	Risk avoidance Risk mitigation Site location	Accidental releases Cleanup of hazardous waste landfills Degree of contamination, presence of endangered species
Natural resource use	Habitat integrity Species introductions	Land use (e.g., road construction, mining, agriculture and logging) Integrated pest management

consider the economic costs and ecological risks that may arise during the manufacture, transportation, use, and disposal of the chemical. Other criteria important in making a decision may include:

- costs and benefits to various stakeholders (business, communities, individuals, etc.),
- human health effects (occupational, nearby residents, etc.),
- ecological effects (populations, communities, ecosystems), and
- ecological effects of not using the chemical.

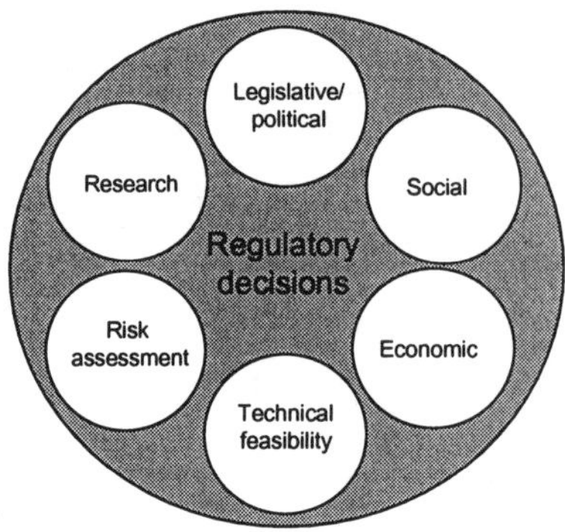

Figure 2-2   Factors influencing a risk management decision

The decision criteria vary for different decision-makers and decisions. For example, a compliance decision made by government may be based on the likelihood of specified health and ecological risks with little or no attention to economic costs. Conversely, most business decisions include some consideration of economic costs. Although methods exist for making tradeoffs among the criteria, in practice these tradeoffs are often subjective judgments made by the decision-maker.

2.3   Interaction between the risk manager and risk assessor

Ecological risk assessment lends support to a risk management decision by evaluating the likelihood of ecological effects caused by human activities as specified by the decision criteria. If the risk manager requires that an ERA be performed, the risk manager and risk assessor begin a dialogue to define the risk assessment problem. Essentially, this step is a translation from the higher-level decision criteria from the manager to a formulation of an evaluation question with specific assessment and measurement endpoints and testable hypotheses. The risk manager and risk assessor first need to define the problem in a management context by answering 6 questions:

1) What management decision will the risk assessment support? (see Table 2-1)

2) What are the time constraints on performing the risk assessment?

3) What is the budget for the risk assessment, including the collection and generation of additional data and/or modeling?

4) Is there going to be more than 1 assessment (i.e., more than 1 alternative to be examined)?

5) What is the maximum level of uncertainty that will still allow for a decision to be made?

6) What are the reference conditions against which possible adverse effects will be compared?

These questions often require numerous iterations before satisfactory answers are obtained. Budgets and time limits are often not explicitly defined initially or are subject to change over time. Further dialogue involving the stakeholders up front in problem formulation may make the assessment endpoints and measurement endpoints understandable and lend credibility to the assessment in the eyes of the stakeholders and the general public. This interaction was highlighted recently in an editorial by Moore and Biddinger (1995).

For example, consider the spotted owl case study. The study is a natural resource management decision relating to habitat integrity. The owls and the loggers both utilize the resources of old and new growth trees in the Pacific Northwest: the owls as habitat for survival, and the loggers as a source of income. The risk assessor needs to examine the age composition and acreage of the forest as they relate to the stability of the owl population, while the economic analyst needs to examine the age composition and acreage as they relate to the number of jobs and profits generated. The economic analyst would have to work with the risk manager and risk assessor in specifying the combinations of age composition and acreage that are currently under consideration for different harvesting plans. The risk assessor would then determine the probability of owl survival within the confidence limits required by the risk manager for each of the specified combinations of age composition and acreage. An economic analysis would also be performed on each of the possible harvesting plans. With this "up-front" coordination, it is then possible to conduct a straight forward cost-benefit analysis during risk management in order to choose the best possible environmental decision.

2.4 Selection of assessment endpoints

At this point, the iterative dialogue between the risk manager and risk assessor has adequately defined the goals for the risk assessment, and the responsibility has shifted to the assessor. The next steps characterize the problem as well as select assessment endpoints that will support the risk management decision.

To arrive at appropriate assessment endpoints, the risk assessor will often consult other experts and information sources to learn about the stressors, ecosystems, and receptors of interest. The characterization begins by identifying the characteristics of the stressor, which include the following:

- type: chemical, physical, or biological;
- intensity: concentration and magnitude;
- duration: short term or long term;
- frequency: single event, episodic, or continuous;
- temporal scale: months, years, or decades; and
- spatial scale: local, regional, national, or global.

Evaluation of properties of the ecosystems at risk is also necessary to characterize the problem. Below are examples of several critical ecosystem properties:

- biotic conditions: types of species, trophic level relationships;
- abiotic conditions: climate, geology, hydrology; and
- land use: historical disturbance patterns, type.

Conducting such a characterization will provide the risk assessor with information that will assist in the selection of ecologically based assessment endpoints needed to support the risk management decision. Examples of assessment endpoints might include the following:

- probability of local extinction,
- probability of reduced production of commercially important species, and
- probability of loss of sensitive habitat.

If the assessment endpoint can be measured directly, there is no need to select measurement endpoints (Barnthouse 1992). More often, however, assessment endpoints cannot be measured directly; thus, there is a need for measurement endpoints. Measurement endpoints include measurable responses to stressors, and several examples are listed below:

- field observations: fish or bird kills, changes in community structure;
- field tests: micro- and mesocosms, caged studies;
- laboratory tests: single species, multiple species; and
- models: fate-and-transport, bioaccumulation, effects.

2.5   Assembling a conceptual model

The conceptual model specifies the hypotheses to be tested during the analysis and risk estimation phases of the ERA. Assembling a conceptual model based on the characterization of the problem and the selection of assessment and measurement endpoints allows the risk assessor to evaluate the effects of a stressor on receptors in the ecosystem at risk. Further, the conceptual model should describe how the assessment will be conducted and the types of data and tools that will be utilized.

The conceptual model is developed by constructing a series of qualitative exposure scenarios that describe how selected ecological receptors could interact with a stressor. A preliminary evaluation of the stressor characteristics, ecosystems at risk, and environmental effects can assist in developing the model. Stressors, geographical scale, temporal scale, biological scale, ecosystem, and system interaction are defined in each scenario. For example, an exposure scenario for a chemical stressor such as 1,1,1-trichloroethane would require information on the following:

- locations and quantities of releases to different media,
- transport processes,
- partitioning behavior between media, including biota,
- physical degradation pathways and rates,
- biodegradation pathways and rates, and
- identification of exposure routes for selected receptors.

2.6 Capabilities and benefits of a decision-support system

At the workshop, the problem-formulation group considered the capabilities that a decision-support system should provide to aid the risk assessor in the problem-formulation phase. As discussed above, the risk manager and risk assessor are often required to have significant interaction at the onset of the problem-formulation phase. This interaction is key to formulating a risk assessment strategy that addresses the risk management question. The workshop participants agreed that a decision-support system should provide the following capabilities:

- documentation of decisions reached during the problem-formulation process,
- guidance through the problem-formulation process via "coaching" drop-down windows and supporting hypertext, and
- visualization and decision-support tools for constructing the conceptual model.

Documentation of the entire formulation process is essential to permit eventual peer review of the risk assessment. Additionally, assessors involved in complex risk assessments will be aided by the ability to document and subsequently revisit the record of decisions made throughout the process. This will allow the assessor to reconstruct various analyses.

Visualization of the conceptual model through computerized decision-analysis tools allows the user the flexibility of creating and modifying the conceptual model on-line as well as the power to design complex multilevel analyses through the use of influence diagrams and fault trees.

The benefits of a coaching system are useful to both the novice and the expert. The novice could find detailed help through hypertext resources and a formalized system to document decisions. The expert would be provided tools to enhance consistency and techniques that would allow the flexibility and the power to modify and iteratively analyze the problem efficiently and effectively.

Chapter 3

Model selection considerations in fate-and-effects analysis

B. Parkhurst, S. Christensen, R. Goldstein, B. Neely, and K. Solomon

The fate-and-effects working group was not charged with describing how to do an analysis. Rather, they were charged with evaluating how a decision-support system would provide technical assistance in any analysis. To that end, the group considered sources of data and models, as well as approaches to document the technical basis for which data and models would be used in an analysis. This section was never intended to be a complete review of the technical criteria for data or model selection; these aspects are only covered here as the workshop attendees felt it appropriate to meet their initial charge. Readers who are looking for such guidance might start with the review by Bartell et al. (1992).

3.1 Overview of fate-and-effects analysis

Fate-and-effects models are being used increasingly in ecological risk assessment (ERA) to characterize the transport, fate, and effects of ecological stressors. These models can be simple descriptions of present concentrations/levels of stressors, mass balance fate models or complex transport, fate, population, and community models. These models may include chemical, biological, and physical components. In addition to their use in risk characterization (see Chapter 4), the problem-formulation stage may need preliminary data and/or model results to aid in the problem formulation and scoping.

Once the problem-formulation phase has been completed, the risk assessor requires 2 types of information to complete the assessment: information on stressor concentrations or other measures of magnitude for non-chemical stressors and information on the potential effects of the stressor, such as its toxicity. This information can be obtained in 2 ways, depending on the type of risk assessment. If the risk assessment is assessing the risks of a stressor that is already present in the environment, empirical measurements can be used to estimate its magnitude and effects. For example, if the stressor is a chemical, then chemical measurements can be made to measure its concentration in the environment, and empirical measurements of ecological populations and communities can be used to estimate the effects of the chemical.

The other way for the risk assessor to gather the information is through non-empirical estimates. Some risk assessments, such as for a new chemical or for an existing chemical for which empirical measurements cannot be made, may rely solely on non-empirical estimates of the magnitude of the stressor and its effects. These non-empirical estimates generally are made using a variety of simple or complex models. This section describes a proposed process for the ecological risk assessment decision-support system (ERADSS) for selecting appropriate models. For the purpose of this section, the term "models" will include methods to estimate stressor magnitude or effects potential based on either empirical measurements or non-empirical techniques.

3.1.1   *Statement of the problem*

To facilitate the risk analysis, problem formulation should produce a quantitative, preferably testable, hypotheses. Such hypotheses should have well-defined spatial and temporal resolution, along with clear delineation of the nature of the ecological stressors. Example hypotheses include the following:

- The use of a pesticide will not cause significant (e.g., 20%) loss in the bass population on a lake located in the same watershed.
- The loss of bass in a lake is proportional to the amount of pesticide used in the watershed.

These statements can be used to produce a conceptual model or diagram illustrating the main components of the assessment (see USEPA 1992).

3.2   Overview of the system

To facilitate the choice of appropriate models and data for fate-and-effects analysis, the conceptual model derived from the problem formulation should address key attributes of the problem at hand, allowing the assessors to suggest an appropriate subset of mathematical or empirical fate-and-effects models among those potentially available (e.g., Figure 3-1). Using the key attributes provided, the ERADSS will indicate which models meet the technical and regulatory criteria for the assessment. This resulting list of analytical tools, including data requirements, will then be compared to the available data to identify which models meet the need of the risk assessment.

3.2.1   *Key attributes*

Topics for the key attributes for model selection include the following:

Stressor: Stressors are the source of ecological risk. Stressors can be chemical, physical, or biological, or combinations of the three. Identification of stressors defines the nature of the activity or the type of chemical substance that can potentially lead to an ecological impact. A risk assessment often encompasses more than a single stressor. The stressor can be defined by multiple attributes, both general and specific. Hence, naphthalene can be defined as both "naphthalene" and "polycyclic aromatic hydrocarbons" (PAHs). The more general keyword permits the

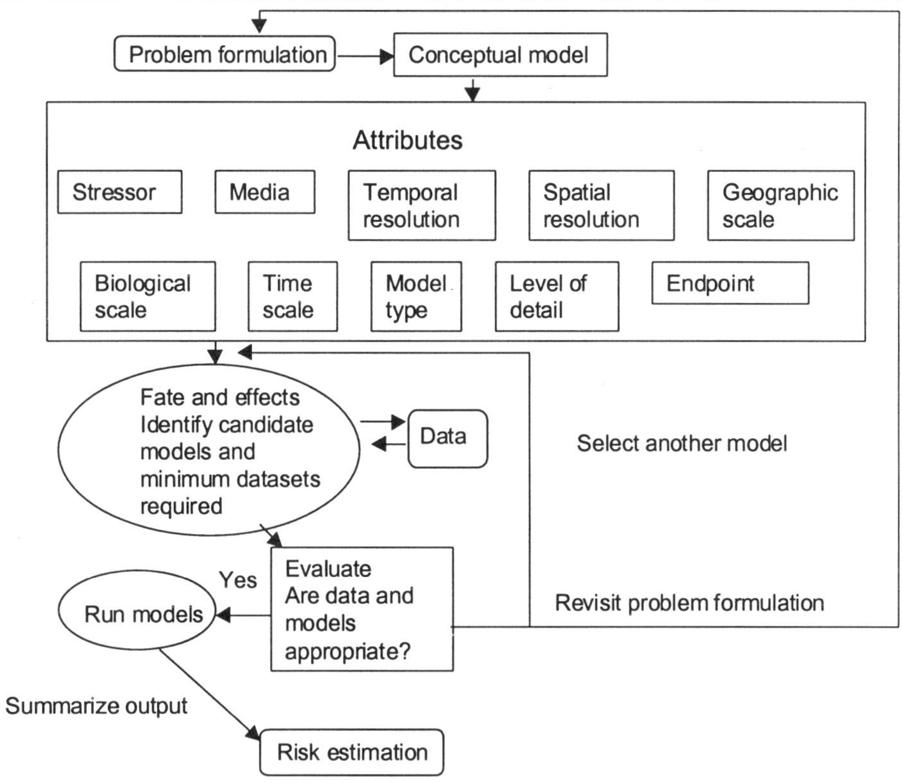

Figure 3-1　　Flow diagram of fate-and-effects models for ERADSS

identification of models that may be relevant to the assessment under consideration as a result of being applied to PAHs other than naphthalene.

Media: The keywords for media also include terms that can range from the very general (e.g., water, soil, air) to a specific situation (e.g., the Hudson River). Hence, a natural progression for a risk assessment involving a specific water body may proceed: water → surface waters → lake → seepage lake → Crystal Lake. A risk assessment can incorporate both multimedia and combinations of biota.

Temporal resolution: Temporal resolution of models may describe the present situation (e.g., in a historically contaminated site) or describe the future (or past) conditions of the system in terms of hourly, daily, weekly, monthly, or annual rates of change. It important that the resolution be chosen to match the properties of the stressor and the ecological impacts.

Spatial resolution: Spatial resolution in the hypothesis (and the model) may range from fixed units or dimensions, such as m^2, km^2, number of soil layers, number of water layers, to compartments in the environment, such as lake strata (e.g., epilimnion or hypolimnion) or soil horizons. Spatial scale also applies to consideration of the stressors and the ecological impacts.

Geographic scale: Hypotheses can be stated pertaining to a specific site, to a region, or to the entire globe. Hypotheses may also include combinations of geographic scales.

Biological scale: Ecological risks can be assessed at different levels of biological organization, ranging from biochemical to individual organisms, populations, communities, ecosystems, and so forth. The hypotheses that comprise the analysis may be stated with respect to any of these levels or any combinations.

Time scale: The time scale associated with the hypothesis may be near-term or long-term. In the latter case, however, it is likely that the uncertainty of the outcome will be more difficult to assess, and evaluating the performance of the model may be equivocal.

Model type: Models may be used to predict chemical fate or effects, or they may combine these 2 processes to predict the movement of a chemical stressor through a food web or food chain.

Level of detail: A tiered approach is generally preferable, beginning with simple screening models and proceeding to more complex models if needed. If a conservative screening model indicates that there is negligible risk, then there may be no need to use more complex, less conservative models.

Endpoints: Endpoints include assessment and measurement endpoints. Assessment endpoints are explicit ecological values that are the focus of the assessment, e.g., the survival rates and productivity of the fish species within a fish community. Measurement endpoints are measurable responses that are directly related to the assessment endpoints, e.g., toxicity of a chemical to fish species that comprise that fish community.

3.2.2   *Using the models for fate-and-effects analysis*

At this point, the selected model is implemented for the scenarios that are required to characterize fate and effects for the problem being evaluated. Then the model outputs are summarized for input into the risk-characterization component. Obtaining results at the end of the process may be as simple as characterizing measured data from a database of field observations or as complex as executing a sophisticated model. If no appropriate model is selected or after data and model evaluation it is decided that the model is unsuitable, the problem-formulation component needs to either redefine the problem or gather additional data required to run the model or answer the question. This would normally require consulting with the risk manager.

3.3   Desirable features for ecological risk assessment decision-support systems

From a fate-and-effects modeling perspective, the design and development of an ERADSS should perform the following functions:

- assist in identifying, accessing, and using models (and other tools) for fate-and-effects analysis;
- provide clear documentation on origin of data or models with original documentation of validation efforts, as appropriate;
- provide regulatory precedence, data availability, and previous model performance (i.e., verification, validation);
- provide a summary of model results in a format consistent with risk-assessment reporting, using terminology understandable to risk assessors and risk managers;
- provide tools for documenting the basis for data or model selection, as well as the inherent strengths and weaknesses (i.e., uncertainty) of the data or models;
- allow the credibility of model results to be evaluated in the context of the current assessment—the results of the evaluation should provide feedback for model selection in future assessments;
- include guidance and tutorials with case examples on model and data selection criteria and model use;
- allow access to a wide range of models;
- provide communication protocols for data access and transfer;
- enhance or facilitate cross-compatibility of models; and
- provide hypertext assistance to the user.

Chapter 4

Risk characterization

J. Lipton, D. Cacela, C. Cowan, P. deFur, L. Ginzburg, and C. Mebane

4.1 Overview of risk characterization

The risk-characterization workgroup evaluated the current, general steps in the risk-characterization process, state-of-the-art in risk characterization, and the potential development of a decision-support system. In addition, the workgroup evaluated lessons learned from the case studies and provided recommendations for developing an ecological risk assessment decision-support system (ERADSS).

4.1.1 Background

The risk-characterization phase of an ecological risk assessment (ERA) involves evaluation, quantification, and interpretation of potential adverse ecological effects, the potential magnitude of those effects, their ecological relevance or significance, and uncertainties associated with any conclusions and/or predictions. The results of this phase can be both quantitative and qualitative. The quantitative aspects of risk characterization serve as the principle focus for the workgroup's discussions and involve taking the results of problem formulation and fate-and-effects analysis to quantify potential adverse effects.

This description of adverse effects can involve many different approaches, including both predictive and retrospective evaluations. Each of the existing approaches currently involves a number of potential drawbacks and/or limitations. For example, assessing risks posed by previous disturbances can be extremely costly, often involving exhaustive site-specific toxicological and ecological research. Moreover, the applicability of such assessments may be limited to "pre-existing conditions" (a limitation in regulatory settings in which the potential for adverse effects must be evaluated). Although the lessons learned from retrospective analyses may be applied, predictively, in different settings, forecasting ecological risks is constrained by an incomplete understanding of ecological systems.

The workgroup evaluated the development of a decision-support system by addressing the following questions:

- What aspects of the ecological risk characterization are amenable to inclusion in a decision-support system?

- How feasible is development of a decision-support system?
- If developed, would such a tool be useful? To whom?
- What are the workgroup's recommended next steps?

4.1.2   Definitions

The following definitions apply for purposes of this chapter:

Risk: the probability of an adverse ecological event.

Expected loss: the product of risk and the magnitude of the adverse event. Some define this product as "risk."

Uncertainty: conditions and factors that introduce variability to risk estimates. Uncertainty can be divided into 2 general classes: natural variability (i.e., stochastic) and incomplete understanding.

4.1.3   Expected results

The results of the risk-estimation process could include quantification of the following:

- risk,
- expected loss, and
- uncertainty bounds for both estimates above (i.e., probability estimates should include variance estimates).

4.1.4   Conceptual flow diagram

The workgroup evaluated possible conceptual flow diagrams for conducting risk characterization. The purpose of this exercise was to formulate a strawman design of a decision-support system. The conceptual flow diagram was intended to be neither comprehensive of all steps in the risk-estimation process nor inclusive of all possible approaches to risk characterization.

The risk-characterization phase of an ERA consists of using the output of the fate/effects/assessment phase (e.g., exposure concentrations, exposure/response models) to estimate risks, expected losses, and associated uncertainties. The workgroup found the division from the fate/effects phase to be somewhat artificial in that the steps involved in risk characterization include executing the integration of the analytical tools and data developed in the other phases of the assessment. Therefore, the generalized flow diagram presented in Figure 4-1 should be viewed as a process closely coordinated with the overall assessment.

4.2   State-of-the-art

The workgroup discussed the current state of the risk-characterization practice. The discussion of available methodologies was not intended to be comprehensive of the full suite of approaches. It is intended to describe and evaluate general "classes" of approaches in order to consider the possibility of including such methodologies in an expert support system. In practice, risk assessors may employ any or all of the methods identified below. The description of adverse effects (risk, expected loss) can involve many different approaches, including both predictive and retrospective (i.e., reconstructive) evaluations.

4.2.1 Retrospective *risk* assessment

Retrospective evaluations can include performing site-specific studies to determine the nature and magnitude of loss. Methodologies for retrospective analyses include the following:

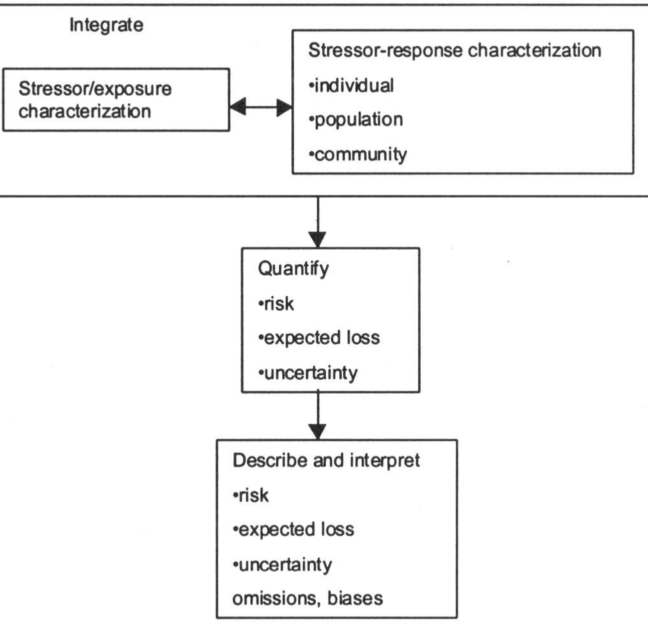

Figure 4-1   General   risk   characterization   flow diagram

- Before-after control-impact analyses (BACI)—Use of the term "control" generally refers to "reference" sites rather than true experimental controls (Stewart-Oaten 1986). The BACI approach involves sampling at both test and reference sites before and after the ecological stress is applied.

- Before-after analyses (impact site only)—This design is similar to the BACI approach except sampling is only undertaken at the impact site (before and after the stress).

- Matched impact-reference analyses—This approach involves sampling at impact sites and matched reference sites (after the stress).

- Within-impact dose-response gradient analyses—This approach involves sampling only within the impact site following the stress along some gradient of expected stress. Stress and response are both quantified along this gradient to infer dose-response relationships.

For each of these methodologies, statistical sampling methods are used to evaluate risk and loss. Often, field sampling to characterize exposure and quantify population effects is coupled with laboratory experimental studies that evaluate stress-response relationships (Figure 4-2).

4.2.2   Predictive risk assessments

Risk-characterization can also involve predictive approaches such as

- comparison of exposure concentrations to adverse effects thresholds (quotient method) (USEPA 1992; EC 1993, 1994);

- simulation modeling to compare distributions of exposures to distributions of adverse effects thresholds (Rodier and Mauriello 1993);

- individual-based modeling to predict responses of individuals using dose-response relationships (Bradbury et al. 1989; DeAngelis and Gross 1992);

- modeling to predict responses based on population dynamics (Bartell et al. 1992);

- population modeling to predict responses based on observed stress-population responses (Ginzburg et al. 1982; Barnthouse 1993; Burgman et al. 1993);

- food-chain modeling (linked trophic levels where each trophic level is equivalent to a population model) (Thomann 1989; Bartell et al. 1992); and

- ecosystem modeling (including food webs, multiple media, ecosystem function/ processes) (Bartell et al. 1992).

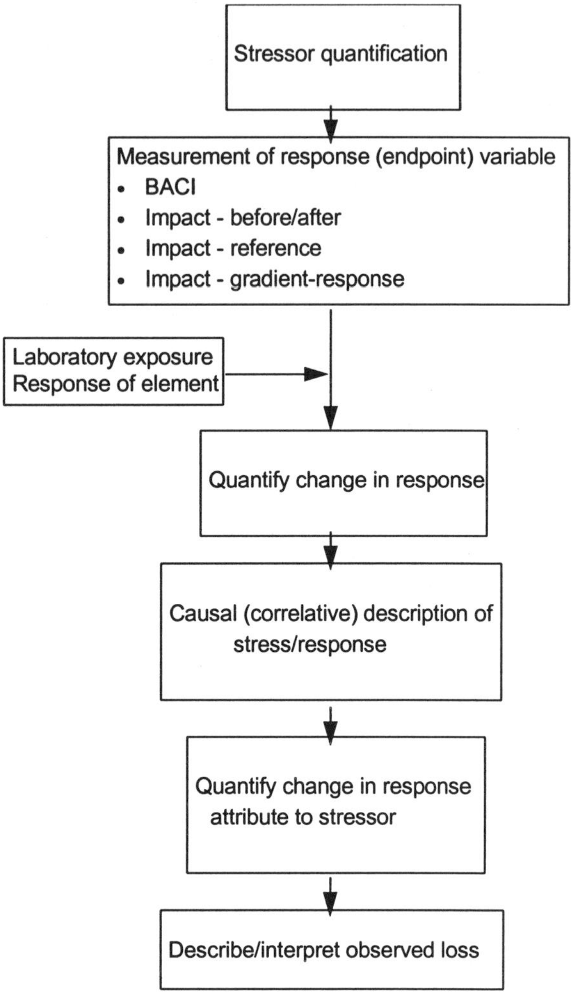

Figure 4-3 provides an example flow diagram for a predictive risk characterization.

Figure 4-2   Example flow diagram for retrospective risk characterization

Of these approaches, the quotient method is currently most commonly used. The methods, as listed from top to bottom, have increasing data needs and increasing difficulty. Most data, particularly historical data, apply to the first 2 approaches. Recent data on standard test species (physiology, toxicology) have been of high quality and support individual-based models well. Although numerical methodologies and models have been developed for population-level estimation, data to support these models (including data on non-standard test species, ecological relationships, and population dynamics) largely do not exist.

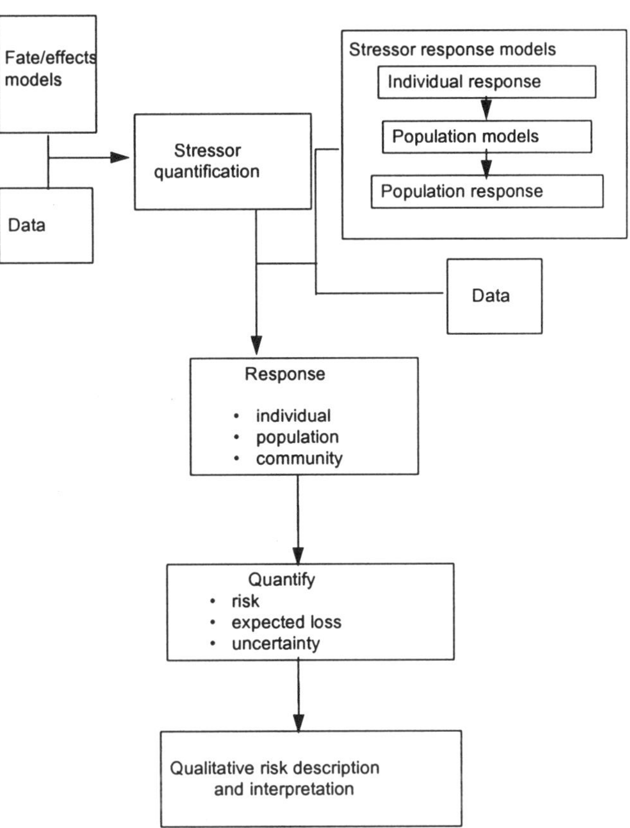

Figure 4-3   Example flow diagram for predictive risk characterization

The risk-characterization phase may need to move beyond the simplified quotient method of calculating an effect per unit loading or effect per incremental change in concentration of a chemical. This need is particularly true for the application of risk assessment and risk estimation to non-chemical stressors (e.g., land use, natural resource use, habitat alteration, and species changes). The improvement gained by identifying a range or a statistical distribution of values is only an improvement in the basic quotient method and not a substantive change in the basic method. Population and/or ecosystem evaluation or modeling is one conceptual approach that is fundamentally different from the quotient method, and we recommend development of such approaches to a usable level. Such systems or models will incorporate data on multiple pathways and compartments within a biological and physical environment. However, usable development of such models will require extensive research and data collection.

Examples of general categories of quantitative uncertainty methodologies (for estimating variability of the risk and expected loss) include the following approaches:

- simple high-medium-low (quartiles, etc.) range-finding analysis;
- Monte Carlo simulation methods, including simple and structured sampling strategies such as Latin hypercube sampling, are an approximate but robust technique for simulating probability distributions of specified shape and (rank) correlation structure (Iman and Conover 1980; Ferson 1994);
- dependency bounds analysis, a numerical method by which bounds on probabilities can be computed when joint distributions are unknown and only marginal distributions are specified (Glaz and Johnson 1984; Ferson and Long 1994); and
- fuzzy arithmetic, a generalization of interval analysis based on possibility theory; analogous to probability theory but applies to non-statistical uncertainty such as measurement error (Kaufman and Gupta 1985; Ferson and Kuhn 1992).

Dependency bounds analysis and fuzzy arithmetic are better formulated to examine the implications of extreme values in assessing risks; combinations of extreme values can result in low frequency/high consequence events. Quantitative uncertainty analysis (in any of the above forms) currently is applied to the minority of ERAs.

4.3   Issues regarding the case studies

The workgroup reviewed the 3 case studies to evaluate any implications for development of a decision-support system. The 3 case studies demonstrate that different risk-characterization methodologies may be required for different types of ecological stresses. For example, the TCA study required predictive modeling; a quotient-type approach was appropriate to addressing the question of whether TCA should be added to the Montreal protocol. The approach to the Commencement Bay study was based on site-reference methods. For the spotted owl study, predictive population modeling was required with the endpoint being the probability of the population level falling below a threshold. Although 2 of the 3 case studies did not include uncertainty analysis (probably a workshop artifact), this would have been desirable and necessary in an actual risk assessment.

The workgroup concluded that the case study exercise pointed to the need for any decision-support system to include multiple methods for risk estimation, as well as multiple methods for uncertainty propagation. The workgroup also concluded that the case studies underlined the diversity of the problems, methods, and approaches in ERAs. Moreover, the case studies demonstrated the current limitations to the state of the practice.

4.4   Development of a decision-support system

Ecological risk assessment is a rapidly evolving, complex process that includes a number of non-quantifiable, interpretive, multi-disciplinary evaluations. As a result, it remains questionable whether a single computerized system capable of supporting the entire ERA process for diverse applications is feasible. The system development is currently constrained both by the diversity of ERA problems and the diversity of data needs. In addition, ERA is an evolving discipline that includes nonquantifiable, interpretive steps that might not be easily captured in a computerized system. It will be particularly challenging to develop a computer system of a practice for which theoretical models are still in early development, and data are unavailable to evaluate many fundamental ecological and toxicological questions.

Chapter 5

Obtaining data for ecological risk assessment

S. Bradbury, J. Hermens, W. Karcher, G. Niemi, R. Purdy, and C. Richards

5.1 Relevance to other ERADSS components

Observations from the case studies indicated that the use of data and data-estimation models are important throughout the risk-assessment process. The data needed to develop a risk assessment include, but are not limited to, physicochemical properties of chemical stressors, exotic species distributions, chemical loadings, land-use patterns, toxic effects information, and species distributions and relative abundance. Several of these data types require Geographic Information System (GIS) technology for efficient handling and incorporation into an ecological risk assessment (ERA). Geographic Information System is essential for 3 integral segments of database function: 1) as a tool for showing the distribution of many parameters (chemical, physical, biological); 2) as a means to store spatially referenced environmental, transport and distribution data; and 3) as a means to extract unique information from separate datasets.

Problem formulation, including definition of the stressors' characteristics, the ecosystems potentially at risk, ecological effects, the determination of assessment and measurement endpoints, and the establishment and refinement of conceptual models is heavily dependent upon existing or readily estimated data within spatial and temporal criteria. During the risk-analysis phase, data can be used directly to characterize ecosystems, or to analyze exposures and ecological responses. In addition, data can be used as inputs to exposure-and-effect models to ultimately establish exposure and stressor-response profiles. In the risk-characterization phase, an understanding of the data quality and the assumptions used in selecting data-estimation techniques are essential components to the uncertainty analysis.

Figure 5-1 depicts how data and data-estimation techniques can be incorporated within the problem-formulation and analysis phases of a risk assessment. Within the problem-formulation phase, data and data-estimation techniques to define stressor characteristics can include databases and quantitative structure-activity relationship (QSAR) models that relate attributes of chemical structure to physical-chemical properties or biological activity, GIS-based chemical-loading and monitoring data, pesticide use patterns, habitat

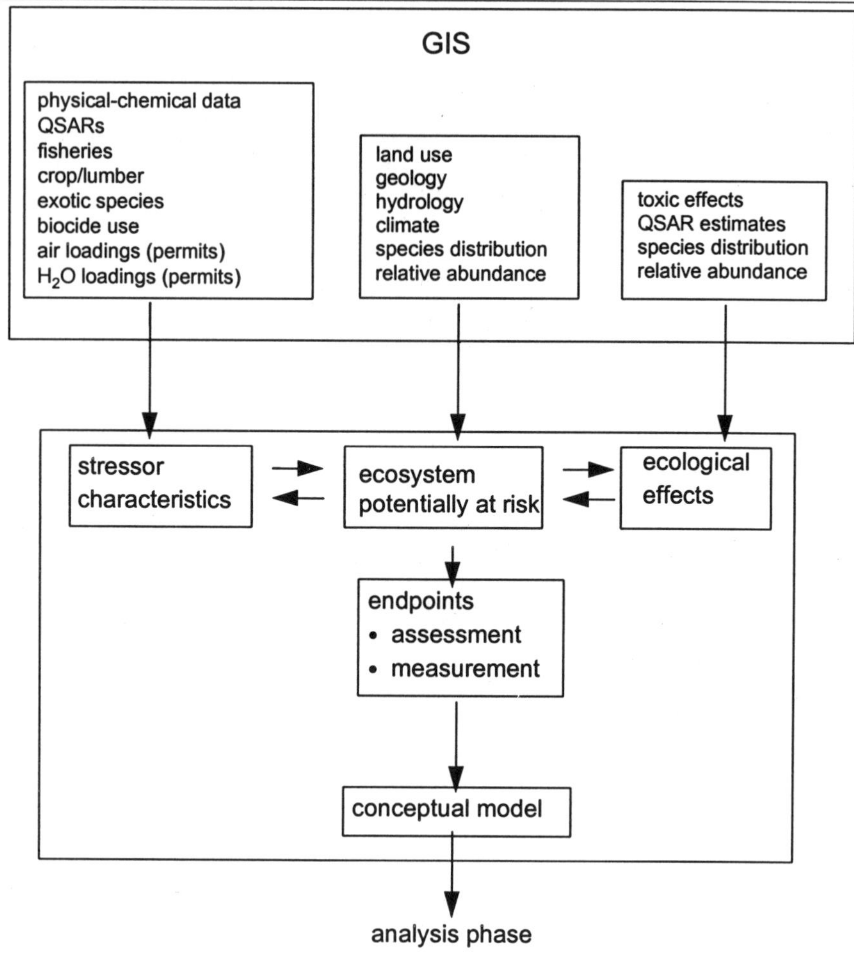

Figure 5-1   Problem formulation

changes, fisheries harvesting patterns, and exotic species distributions and habitat specificity.

Data that may be used to establish ecosystems potentially at risk could include land-use cover and geographically referenced geology, hydrology, and climatology information. These data may be used to delineate the ecosystem in question. The spatial and temporal scales of interest will depend on the questions being posed. These data define the media and background for formulating assessment endpoints. All of these data have explicit spatial and temporal definitions that must be retained in the data structure.

Information available for establishing potential ecological effects includes toxic effect databases for aquatic life, wildlife, and terrestrial plants, as well as related QSAR systems. Additional databases would consist of basic information on the biology of plant and animal organisms, populations, and communities. Ideally, these databases (if available) could consist of the following: 1) species distribution, relative abundance, and GIS-based trends; 2) life history characteristics including reproduction parameters (e.g., generation time and fecundity), growth rates, and habitat specificity; 3) species physiology (e.g., respiration rates, etc.); and 4) species status and vulnerability (e.g., endangered, threatened, special concern, or economic value). Higher levels of biological organization could also be included such as food web relationships, community structure (e.g., species diversity, evenness, and biomass), as well as indices that describe biological diversity and integrity, or other ecosystem properties (i.e., decomposition or production rates).

During the analysis phase, the same data and data-estimation techniques are incorporated in the characterization of exposure and effects. In some instances, these data can serve as the primary information used to undertake the exposure and ecological response analyses (e.g., a new chemical risk assessment), while in other situations these data may serve as inputs (e.g., stressor characterization, ecosystem characterization, evaluation of effects data) to higher level exposure and ecological response models. Available data and associated QSARs can be used to supply data to perform worst-case estimates with simple models. The results can be used to indicate whether more complex and expensive data gathering is needed. For example, if an acceptable outcome is seen in a worst-case analysis, no further effort may be required. Also, the results of worst-case analyses can indicate the kind of data needed for a more extensive evaluation.

The characteristics of data used in a risk assessment also impact the uncertainty analysis undertaken in the risk-characterization phase of the assessment. The extent to which actual data or models are used to provide the information needed to establish the exposure and effects profiles contributes to an evaluation of assessment uncertainties.

5.2　Sources of data for ecological risk assessment

In the sections that follow, a limited number of sources for data relating to stressors, environmental characteristics, and effects are provided. These references are in no way an exhaustive list of sources for such data; they are merely representative sources that were identified by the workshop participants.

5.2.1　*Data describing the stressor*

With regard to chemical stressors, there are several databases available for physical-chemical and fate properties. However, few of these databases contain information on methodology and estimates of variance. For example, an ideal description would include the mean, a variance estimate (e.g., standard error or standard deviation), and the sample size (n) of the experimental unit used to calculate these statistics. In the context of consistency, databases providing information derived with standard methodology are generally preferred. In addition, those databases that provide the primary reference citations are especially useful because they permit the means to verify the reported data and associated methodology. Some currently available databases permit the user to select data based on specified quality characteristics.

Several databases in support of regulatory activities have been established within Europe and North America, including

- International Unified Chemicals Information Database (IUCLID), managed by the European Chemicals Bureau, JRC Ispra, European Commission;
- Chemical Evaluation Search and Retrieval System (CHEMINFO and CESARS), managed by the Ontario Ministry of the Environment and Michigan Department of Natural Resources; and
- ATSDR HAZDAT database (Hazardous Substance Release/Health Effects Database).

In addition, several commercially supported databases are also available. These databases, maintained in both PC and mainframe environments, contain information such as octanol-water partition coefficient, melting point, boiling point, vapor pressure, heat of vaporization, aqueous solubility, dissociation constant, bioconcentration factor, organic carbon-water partition coefficient, Henry's Law constant, and biodegradation rate.

To some extent, data gaps may be filled with the application of QSARs; several systems are available. Some systems are designed for the nonexpert user and provide reasonable documentation. The input of chemical structures into both databases and modeling systems can be done in several ways. Although there are no standard methods for structure entry, there are programs that can convert these different input files and formats. Those QSAR systems that provide assumptions, boundaries for reliability (domain) and applicability, and error estimates associated with predictions are preferred.

As an example, the U.S. Environmental Protection Agency's (USEPA) ASTER system (Russom et al. 1991) supplies estimates for octanol-water partition coefficient (CLOGP), water solubility, pK_a, vapor pressure, boiling point, and an indication of biodegradability. For nongovernmental users, commercially supported programs supplying this information are also available.

Uncertainty in data estimation from the above-mentioned models is of 2 types:

- the reliability of the model itself (e.g., standard error of estimate, which is usually available), and
- the choice of the correct model.

In particular, the second issue is of primary importance and points to the need for defining the domain of a model.

The availability of information on physical or biological stressors varies widely. For many situations, such as logging activity or land use changes, current information (e.g., annual information) is unlikely to be available. With the development and advancement of remote sensing techniques, this need is rapidly becoming a reality. Other types of information likely vary considerably depending on the expertise and monetary resources available for the municipality, state, or region. For instance, some cities or states have readily available, geo-referenced data on the use of pesticides, crop production, or logging activity, while others have only crude records. The entire field of information management and the use of GIS are rapidly changing at a variety of organizational levels. Any simple summaries of current data gaps would immediately be outdated.

It is very important that any system developed allows for inclusion of information by the user because of data gaps. This will apply to all parts of the system where information is required.

5.2.2   Data characterizing the environment

The following types of data are useful in characterizing environmental conditions during a risk assessment:

Ecosystems —There is currently rapid development of several central repositories of environmental data (e.g., Consortium of International Earth Science Information Networks [CIESIN]) which are available through the Internet and range widely in topics and specificity. These and other available data are summarized in USGS (1993a).

Land cover —There are several computer-accessible databases that are available. However, they are usually specific to a few countries or regional areas, and spatial and temporal detail is limited. Maps of land cover and remotely sensed data are available for most locations in the world (e.g., LANDSAT). However, most remotely sensed data have not been classified and stored for use in a meaningful way. Several extensive digitized data sets are available for the U.S. (e.g., USGS 1986).

Geology — Surface geology and general geological structure of most regions are well documented. For the most part, data are not readily available for integration in GIS systems at small spatial scales required for many site assessments. Usually, individual countries maintain indexes to regional areas (e.g., STATSGO 1993; USGS 1993b).

Hydrology — In the U.S., complete digitized hydrography is available for over 80% of the country. Most areas of the world are mapped, but this information is not computerized. River-flow data for most countries are incomplete with spotty temporal and spatial coverage. In the U.S., river-flow data are computer accessible from representative regional locations (e.g., USGS 1993c, 1993d).

Climate — General information is readily available for some parts of the world. For instance, the U.S. National Weather Service maintains records for hundreds of stations across the U.S. These data, as well as many other databases, are available through NOAA (1993).

Contaminants — Data describing the concentrations of various contaminants in air, surface water, and groundwater are available on-line from several databases supported by the USEPA (e.g., STORET), USGS, and several states and other countries, such as Canada's Envirodat.

5.2.3   Ecological effects data

Databases for biological characteristics of organisms, populations, and communities are found in widely varying states of sophistication and detail. Probably the most advanced and usable databases are for toxic effects data for individual species and include such databases as AQUIRE, PHYTOTOX, TERRETOX (maintained by USEPA and distributed by both governmental and commercial sources), and IUCLID (maintained by the European Commission and distributed by both governmental and commercial sources). These databases have largely been acquired through systematic and careful review of the literature, and many contain multiple point-estimate values with variance parameters in which uncertainty in the values could be explicitly analyzed or incorporated into models. As previously mentioned, summary statistics that include explicit variance estimates can be used to propagate errors in ecological models. These data would also aid in model use when covariation among variables needs to be considered or in the handling of spatial autocorrelation issues. Those databases that provide the primary reference citations are especially useful because they permit the user the means to verify the reported data and associated methodology.

Experimental data for ecotoxicity are available for only a few species, and little information is available on species-to-species and effects extrapolation, although there is certainly a need for such information. In addition, most database systems do not provide dose-response data, but, through the citations provided, the user is readily directed to the primary literature. Recently, efforts at Oak Ridge National Laboratory have addressed the establishment of a database containing dose-response data for chemicals associated with U.S. Department of Energy (USDOE) facilities (USDOE 1994).

Several QSAR programs are available that supply predictions of ecotoxicity. The previously mentioned ASTER system, other USEPA and European Union systems, as well as several commercial programs, supply estimates for acute toxicity, and in some cases subchronic toxicity, primarily for aquatic life. Quantitative structure-activity relationships for predicting subchronic and chronic toxicity are much less well-established than predictive models for acute toxicity. The same remarks concerning uncertainty and optimal use made for QSARs for physical-chemical and fate properties are valid for ecotoxicity models.

Species distributions and relative abundance are generally known for most vertebrate groups and vascular plants. However, knowledge of smaller organisms and those from "lower" levels of organization is scarce. Unfortunately, digitized data for easy use in modeling efforts, even for distributions, have not been systematically completed except for a few groups (e.g., game animals or some birds) or for selected areas. Trend information also is available for selected species (e.g., game species), but historical records beyond the past 20 to 25 years are virtually nonexistent, again except for a few isolated cases. Perhaps through the creation of the U.S. National Biological Survey, development of these data will be available in the future.

Information about basic life history and physiological characteristics is available for many groups of organisms, especially vertebrates and vascular plants. This knowledge tends to be limited for smaller organisms such as bacteria, protozoans, and insects. In fact, there are millions of species that still need to be described, many of which occur in well-populated areas of Europe and North America. Even though much of this information is known for the most popular groups and is published in a variety of peer-reviewed and gray literature sources, little data have been systematically compiled in computerized formats. The quality of this information, however, is likely to be quite high for many characteristics.

A variety of information has been developed for species designated as endangered or threatened in North America and in Europe. These organisms would likely represent species of high priority and of immediate concern in ERA. The development of means to assess vulnerability is in the early stages. Most approaches use combinations of species range, relative abundance, habitat specificity, and trends in population to describe vulnerability. Identification of these species and incorporation into GIS databases would be another high priority for ERA.

Other data for higher levels of organization at the community or ecosystem level are in the early stages of development, and little comprehensive information is available in a readily usable format. A number of derived variables based on existing predictive models are available for many characteristics, and these might be used for crude ecological assessments. Among these characteristics are production rates for plants, species-richness maps for breeding bird species, or crude indexes of biotic integrity.

5.3   State-of-the-art

Geographic Information Systems represent a rapidly growing and changing technology. Numerous systems (both public domain and private) exist for storing, relating, and retrieving spatially and temporally referenced data. Although software and hardware systems associated with this technology are still evolving, several standards have emerged. The reasons that these systems have not been extensively used is that scientists and managers lack understanding of GIS capabilities. Technology and the availability of databases are improving rapidly. Until government agencies and private organizations routinely enter geographically referenced data, this information will remain largely unavailable.

In addition to a description of stressor, ecosystem, and effect databases and models, there is also a need for the establishment of a database of ERAs. With such a system, a risk assessor could determine whether a similar assessment has been completed and the extent to which it can be applied to the immediate issue. Initial attempts to collect such information can be found in recent USEPA publications of ERA case studies (USEPA 1993, 1994). However, rather than being an exhaustive compilation of completed assessments, this effort is designed only to provide risk assessors with examples of approaches.

5.4   Data needs for ERADSS development

Compiling existing databases and modeling systems that include results of previous risk assessments and information concerning stressors, ecosystem characterization, and ecological effects data would be a massive and perhaps impossible task. It was recommended that the group not consider this type of an effort during this workshop. Rather, if an ERA modeling/decision-support system is to be developed, participating units should define the realm of stressors, ecosystems, and organisms within their spatial and temporal range of responsibilities. Each unit would then be responsible for acquisition and maintenance of data within their realm. Their participation and potential use would require that these data be available, compatible, and consistent with the system. The design of the system should include adequate feedback with existing database managers, and the system should be designed specifically to include spatially and temporally referenced data.

Risk assessors may find indexes to specific categories of databases useful for rapid problem formulation, as well as analysis and characterization phases of an assessment. Essentially, the establishment of a "database of databases" is envisioned. An effort in this regard is currently being undertaken by the Society for Environmental Research in Munich for chemical stressor related issues. An overall database of databases and estimation modeling systems could be organized by stressor class, ecosystem characteristics, and effects. Indexes could also contain information concerning data extent, type, and quality. A series of workshops for specific categories of databases and associated models (e.g., stressor characteristics, ecosystems, and ecological effects) may be required to accomplish this task in a systematic and orderly fashion. Moreover, the system should include an indexing system that tracks where and what types of data are available at participating units and how the information is made available to facilitate judgment of quality and uncertainty. This database should contain all relevant systems; however, inclusion would require descriptions of scope, including data quality characteristics. For model systems, definition of assumptions, domain, strengths, weaknesses, and data input and output characteristics should be included. It is also suggested that a peer-review panel be established to review and approve descriptions of database or modeling systems prior to their inclusion in the system.

To interface with an overall risk-assessment system, many of the database and modeling systems should be housed in a form that facilitates data exchange. A number of database, model, and GIS protocols exist for easy exchange or access of information. Provisions should be made to include distributed systems (i.e., systems where databases and software reside on physically different platforms that are integrated to provide the user "seamless" access to information and models). Limited experience to date suggests that the Internet likely will serve as a useful mechanism for linking information systems and users. This information exchange tool may provide a means for both storing and retrieving lists of more detailed data sources that may require further review or processing. In addition, data sources that are already compiled and meet listing requirements can be accessed by methods such as file transfer protocols.

Chapter 6

Model testing and evaluation

A. Venkatram, L. Burns, C. Chen, J. Irwin, and M. Johnson

6.1 Overview and relevance to ecological risk assessment decision-support system

The objective in ecological risk assessment (ERA) is to use available stressor and ecological information to estimate the probability that some undesired ecological event will occur (Wilson and Crouch 1987). This estimation usually requires the use of exposure and effects models. Because few of these models have undergone evaluation with observations, the estimates from these models are usually associated with uncertainty. The risk measures resulting from the application of these models are typically stated as point estimates. Point estimates are not couched in terms of the probability of exceeding a specified hazard value. The situation can be improved through a systematic evaluation of ecorisk models to determine the uncertainty in their estimates. This allows expression of risk in terms of the probability of exceeding a specified effects level. This chapter discusses model evaluation and testing procedures that can be incorporated into an ecological risk assessment decision-support system (ERADSS).

6.2 Characterizing uncertainty

Risk assessment is basically a decision analysis tool developed to provide an objective means of comparing the differences between options under consideration. It is important to incorporate uncertainty characterization into the risk assessment process to help us understand the relationship between a predicted exposure and the associated concentration of concern.

Consider a predicted exposure of 7 µg/L of a chemical species being compared to a level of concern of 8 µg/L. Given this point estimate, we are not in a position to state that no impacts will occur. If the uncertainty in the model estimate is ± 2 µg/L (95% C.I.), there is a finite probability that the level of concern will be exceeded. If the same impact is estimated with a model having a greater uncertainty interval, the probability of impact (risk) would be larger. This example points to the importance of associating an uncertainty estimate with a predicted exposure level.

When comparing the differences between 2 estimated outcomes, the characterization of uncertainty provides an objective means for assessing the significance of the observed difference. Consider an assessment in which there are 2 options. The final risk assessment for option 1 estimates there to be a mean loss of 50% of the bird population, while option 2 estimates there to be a mean loss of 65%. Without further information characterizing the uncertainty in these estimates, it is not possible to assess in an objective manner whether these 2 estimates are significantly different. If the variance in the estimated means is 30%, then it can be demonstrated that these estimates cannot be characterized with confidence as being significantly different. If the variance around the means is 15%, however, then it is likely that the difference between the estimated means is significant. For clarity in this discussion, we have avoided references to the various formal statistical tests that would be used in an actual application.

In the examples discussed, the benefit of having less uncertainty in the estimated outcomes is the ability to ascribe certainty to differences seen in projected outcomes. Although the examples illustrate the basic tenet for desiring characterization of modeling uncertainty, the examples may not typify the most frequent potential use of uncertainty in risk assessments.

In more refined modeling applications employing Monte Carlo methods, the modeled total expected losses (cumulative) can be compared among decision options. The total loss is computed by summing over all expectations. Now the uncertainty in the cumulative frequency distributions of possible outcomes becomes important. Consider, for example, 2 options in which the cumulative mean loss over all possible outcomes is equal. In this instance, if the decision is to minimize possible loss, then the option having larger uncertainty in the cumulative frequency distribution of loss is less desirable.

The above discussion is not meant to be comprehensive but is offered to illustrate that if uncertainty in the modeling results is available, so are the means for discerning differences in possible decision alternatives (e.g., Finkel 1990).

6.3   Current practice

In recognition of the uncertainty in currently used ecological models, the ERA modeling community often uses models that are designed to represent only a "reasonable worst-case" scenario. These conservative models are constructed by using inputs that generate impacts expected to be much higher than normal. The U.S. Environmental Protection Agency (USEPA) provides guidance on the process (USEPA 1994). The use of models in this manner is usually referred to as screening; the underlying idea is to identify stressors in need of further risk assessment, with little chance of false negatives. In the case of chemicals, the estimate from such a model is compared with a "concentration of concern," which itself is some fraction of a measured hazard level. This fraction, which ranges from 1/10 to 1/1000, is a function of the uncertainty in the hazard data.

If a new chemical does not pass the screen, the concern level against which the model estimate is compared can be made higher by obtaining better estimates of the hazard level. At some point in this sequential screening approach, the assumption of conservativeness in the model breaks down, and it becomes necessary to use a refined model to better account for the underlying mechanisms. Note that none of these screening models considers uncertainty explicitly.

Because the refined model is not conservative, it is necessary to evaluate the model with observations before it can be used, in addition to primary testing to confirm correspondence with the physical assumptions mechanized in the model (Burns 1983). This evaluation also provides the uncertainty estimates required for decision-making that better accounts for uncertainty. The next section describes one possible approach to the procedure, and the reader should be aware that there are alternative methods (e.g., Faber et al. 1992).

6.4   Quantifying model uncertainty

In order to characterize the performance characteristics of a model, it is necessary to develop a framework that relates a model estimate to the corresponding observation (Burns 1986). Every observation can be expressed as a function of 2 sets of variables:

- α = set of variables used as model inputs; and
- β = set of variables that affect the observation but are not included in the model inputs.

As one potential method we can relate the observation, $C_o(\alpha,\beta)$, to the model prediction, $C_p(\alpha)$, as follows (Venkatram 1982, 1983):

$$C_0\,(\alpha,\,\beta) = C_p\,(\alpha) + \varepsilon(\alpha,\,\beta), \hspace{3cm} \text{Equation   6-1}$$

where $\varepsilon(\alpha,\beta)$ is the residual between model estimate and observation, which occurs because we have not included β in the model estimate. In principle, the residual $\varepsilon(\alpha,\beta)$ can be made smaller by including more of β into the model input set α.

The performance characteristics of a model are then determined by the statistics of the residual:
- $<\varepsilon>^\beta$, average over all possible β for a given α, and
- $<\varepsilon^2>^\beta$, variance of the residual.

The objective of model improvement is to minimize the values of these statistics in the sense

$$<\varepsilon>^\beta \ll C_p \hspace{3cm} \text{Equation 6-2a}$$

and

$$<\varepsilon^2>^\beta \ll \text{variance of } C_p \hspace{3cm} \text{Equation 6-2b.}$$

Equation 6-2a tells us that the mean of the residuals between model estimates and observations is small compared to the model estimate, which is equivalent to the statement that the model bias is small. Equation 6-2b says that the average variance of the residuals is much smaller than the range of model estimates used in the problem at hand. This property allows us to distinguish between 2 model predictions of interest; this is not possible if the average variance is large.

In order to estimate the statistics of the residual, it is necessary to assume that the statistics of the residual are independent of the model inputs. This, then, allows us to estimate the statistics from a pair of model estimates and observations depicted in Figure 6-1.

Then,

$$\langle \epsilon \rangle = \frac{1}{N} \sum_{i=1}^{N} (C_{oi} - C_{pi})$$

Equation 6-3a

and

$$\langle \epsilon^2 \rangle = \frac{1}{N} \sum_{i=1}^{N} (C_{oi} - C_{pi})^2$$

Equation 6-3b.

6.5   Application of model statistics

Once we know the statistics of the residuals, we can simulate an observation using the Monte Carlo step,

$$C_o = C_p + \varepsilon$$

Equation 6-4

where ε is a random variable sampled from the known distribution of residuals, and the model estimate C_p is varied by changing the model inputs over the range of input uncertainty. Notice that if the variance of residuals is large compared to the range of model predictions, the variance of the simulated observations will correspond to that of the residuals. This is equivalent to saying that the model has no value in the analysis.

This Monte Carlo procedure allows us to estimate a distribution of simulated observations over the range of model estimates we are interested in. This distribution of observations can be used in a risk assessment/management approach that incorporates uncertainty.

The use of a model (see Figure 6-1) in this manner suggests that the model that is incorporated into the risk management system should be accompanied by

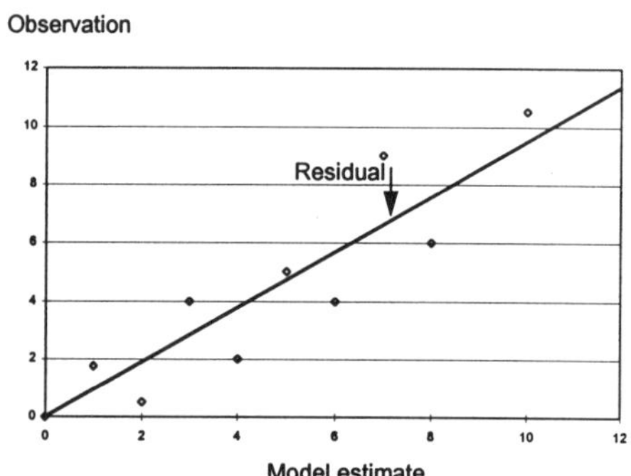

Figure 6-1   Example scatterplot of model estimates and observations to establish model performance

- distribution of residuals, and
- distribution of model inputs.

6.6 Data needs

Data needs exist in 3 categories: 1) information about model performance, 2) input data, and 3) observed data. Usually, uncertainty estimates for models are not reported. Thus, it will be necessary to obtain detailed information on the evaluation of these models to quantify the required residual statistics. Such information might not be readily available. If the selected model has not been evaluated, it is necessary to conduct a field study or to use information on the performance characteristics of a similar model.

The favored method of quantifying model uncertainty is to compare model results to observed data. In many cases, observed data are not available. A robust strategy needs to be developed for these situations. For example, instead of relying on statistical techniques to fabricate variance, one alternative is to use a surrogate for which observed data and/or a model exist. The surrogate data and model can be used to calculate the variance for performance evaluation. Or, one might assume a conservative coefficient of variance (e.g., at least 100%) for the model output values.

6.7 Model evaluation

The preceding description of model performance can be converted into a step-by-step process which includes the following components:

Model selection — Given a library of documented and viable models, one or more models can be selected using selection criteria defined in the problem-formulation phase of the analysis. An alternative would be to use available data that provide a basis for expressing a relationship for characterizing exposures or effects.

Model performance and uncertainty — The next step in the process is to determine whether model evaluation statistics are available. If not, an analysis must be performed, as discussed earlier, to specify the evaluation statistics. There is a benefit to requiring public access to model evaluation datasets. This allows their use in all succeeding performance evaluations. In this manner, the performance-evaluation measures reflect a composite and provide a robust characterization of expected performance. If new model evaluation data are collected on-site, these data are added to all previously employed evaluation datasets to develop a new composite description of model performance. There are standard statistical methods for employing data from disparate field studies, e.g., an inverse variance weighting can be used to define the composite performance measures.

Model-input data — The next step in the process is to determine whether model-input data, representative for the problem specified, are available having a suitable duration and extent for the envisioned assessment. If such data are not available, then these data may be obtained or estimated with assumptions clearly defined.

> In some cases a more simplistic model, requiring less data, can be used; however, the increased uncertainty will need to be considered and explained to the risk manager.
>
> Input-data uncertainty — Input data are acceptable only when accompanied with a description of uncertainty. If such data descriptors are not available, an assessment must be performed to specify the data uncertainty descriptors.

At this point in the process, we have both a suitable model (with specified uncertainty) and a set of representative model input data (with specified uncertainty). This process can be incorporated into the proposed ERADSS.

6.8   Discussion of case studies

In each of the 3 case studies discussed, there was little opportunity for these issues to be addressed. No specific models were suggested, and so it was not possible to address questions of performance or uncertainty. Consequently, our discussions centered on the role of model evaluation in the risk-assessment process. Much of the evaluation of performance and propagation of uncertainty should be performed by the model developers or users before the model is entered into the toolbox. Performance is often evaluated, but personal experience of group members indicates that sensitivity analyses of complex models are seldom performed. Consequently, there is little understanding of the uncertainties associated with the models.

Chapter 7

Design of an ecological risk assessment decision-support system

E. Webb, A. Borison, M. Evans, R. Hunter, H. Jones, and P. Kaplan

7.1 Environmental risk management process

Ecological risk assessment (ERA) is one key part of the process of environmental risk management. This process involves 3 major groups of participants:

- stakeholders,
- risk managers, and
- risk assessors.

Each group has a specific role in this process. The process typically starts and ends with stakeholders who may be from public agencies, private firms, special interest groups, or other organizations. They are responsible for identifying a potential environmental problem and for determining whether it has been resolved. In this process, they interact primarily with risk managers. Risk managers, in turn, are responsible for formulating the environmental problem and for developing recommendations based both on technical and value considerations. They interact both with stakeholders and with risk assessors. Risk assessors are responsible for the technical evaluation of ecological risk. They interact primarily with risk managers.

Figures 7-1 and 7-2 provide a road map that can be used to guide this process. The activities and interactions of each participant are described in more detail in the preceding "component" group discussions.

7.2 Ecological risk assessment process

The development of a decision-support tool for ERA is dependent upon an understanding of the underlying process used by practitioners. The process can either embody actual day-to-day (descriptive) activities, or it can represent an idealized (prescriptive) approach to the problem. One of the objectives of this workshop was to investigate potential approaches, select 1 or merge several, and develop a relatively detailed description of the composite. The process depicted in the diagram is a result of this workshop. Previous sections of this document have described in detail the subcomponents of this proposed approach. Application of this process provides the user several desired products: consistency, accuracy, and eventually efficiency. It also provides a common foundation for communication of risk assessment activities. The addition of a software tool to support either a portion or all of these activities fosters the application of a consistent approach.

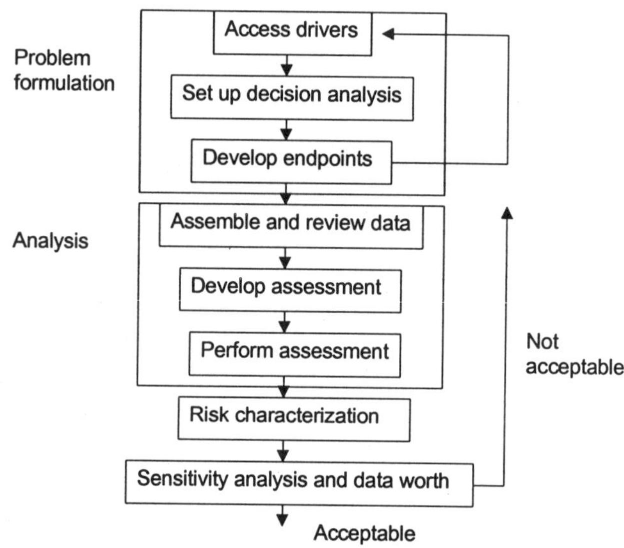

Figure 7-1   Simplified version of ecological risk assessment decision-support process

There are several aspects of the diagram that must be understood:

1) These steps are followed for all types of analyses whether they are for rapid screening analysis or for detailed simulation activities. However, the level of effort expended in each box will vary by problem and by the number of iterations through the problem.

2) The process allows for probabilistic analysis. While the process supports deterministic (single estimate) analytical approaches, it is capable of explicitly dealing with probabilistic/stochastic descriptions of the uncertainty in both the risk assessment and in the risk management components.

3) The boxes indicate who has responsibility for the work. However, this does not preclude the interaction between stakeholders, the manager, the assessor, and the data management team at any point in the process.

The process described above may be used iteratively. Each loop of the iterative process is actually initiated by the stakeholders and managers who, in conjunction with the risk assessor, evaluate the results of each iteration of the process and suggest additional activities to either refine the current analysis or answer follow-up questions. The amount of energy expended on each iteration is determined beforehand and varies from iteration to iteration. The key is that as the risk assessor presents the results of work to the manager, he must be able to present information regarding the completeness of the analysis, describe and evaluate the assessment results, and justify any need for more information. To address these last 2 issues, the assessor might perform some form of sensitivity and data-worth analysis, even if the analysis is qualitative.

The following sections provide specific recommendations for the development of a deci-sion-support system. A basis to access feasibility and several potential philosophies for application and development of the system are reviewed. These suggested approaches are followed by specific recommendations on developing a decision-support system in section 7.6.

7.3 Feasibility assessment

In this section, we discuss the feasibility of the postulated computer system in terms of both the concept and its development. The feasibility assessment asks the questions, "How likely is the proposed endeavor to succeed? Are the benefits of the system sufficient to justify the costs of the assembly of the system?"

There are 5 basic categories of feasibility against which the system concept and develop-ment must be evaluated:

- technical — would it work, and can it be built?
- financial — would the cost of development and use be supported? who would pay for it? would it be used?
- political — would it be accepted by the regulatory community? can this tool fit with current organizational approaches to addressing ecological risk?
- organizational — can satisfactory and practical arrangements be set up both for performing and managing the project?
- legal — can all of the political, financial, and organizational details be legally specified and accepted by all parties?

The reason a feasibility assessment is important is that it is clearly desirable to have a good idea of the chances and mechanisms of success of such a project before pursuing it. The feasibility assessment also provides a checklist of all the relevant issues affecting success, plus it identifies the potential pitfalls and ingredients for success.

The feasibility assessment can provide valuable input to the business plan for the project as it evolves, and should therefore be revisited regularly.

Checklists of the issues arising in each category, which may affect feasibility, are pre-sented below. This is not intended to be a comprehensive list, but instead gives the flavor of questions that must be addressed by this type of analysis.

The following items make up the technical feasibility checklist:

- Does the scientific framework/procedure exist, and how systematic is it?
- Do the tools or theory exist, or can they be developed?
- Is there sufficient information to establish the system?
- Are there adequate hardware and software platforms on which to build the prod-uct?

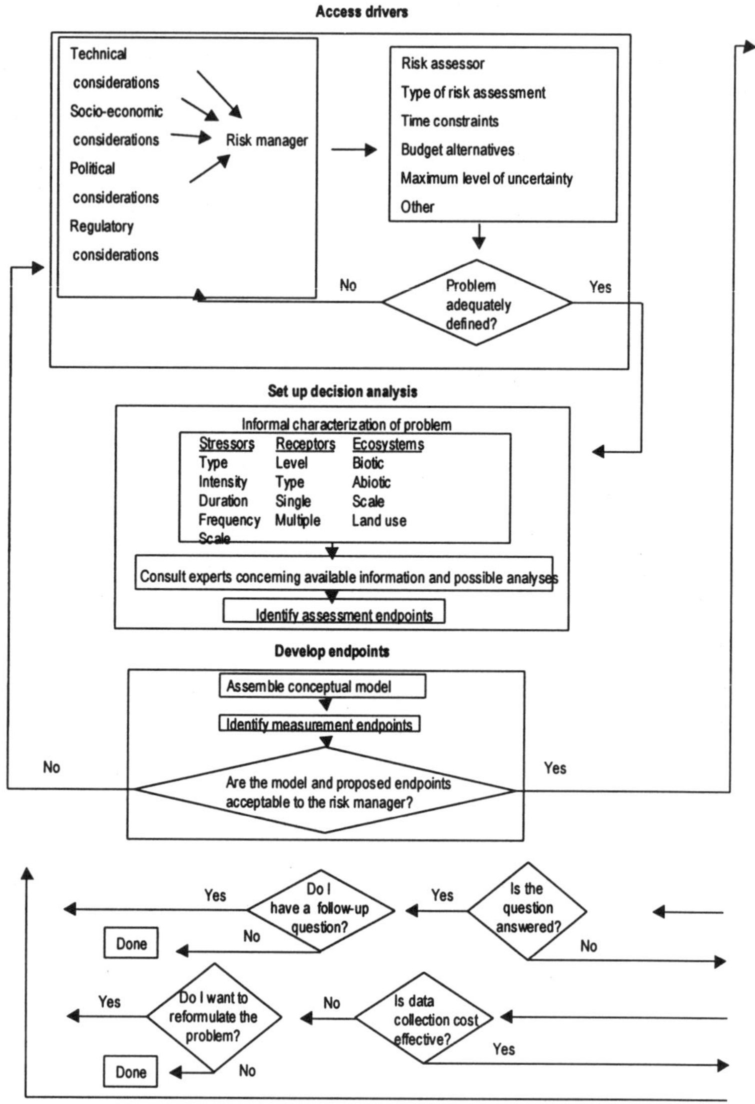

Figure 7-2   Detailed version of ecological risk assessment decision support process

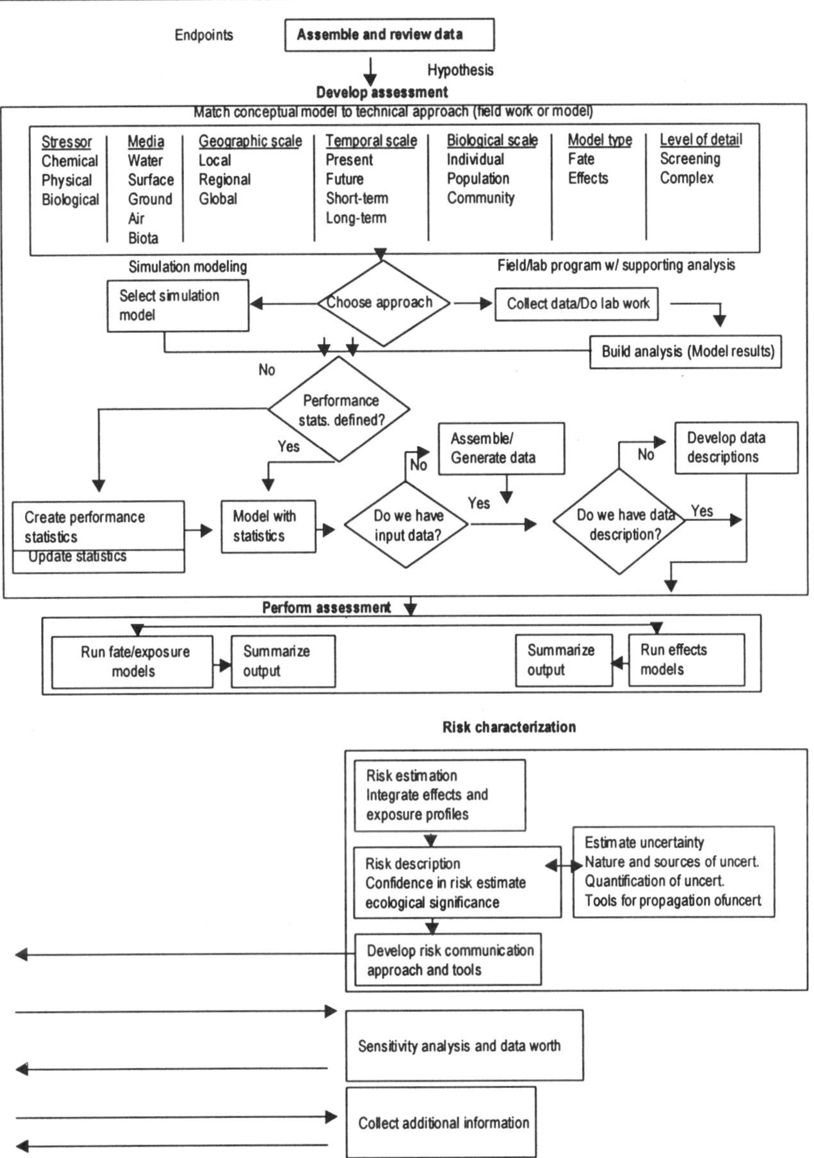

Figure 7-2   continued

- Can prospective users access the hardware/software platforms needed to run the product?

The following items make up the legal feasibility checklist:

- What funding arrangements are allowable?
- Who would own the final product?
- Are there any liability issues for SETAC, developers, etc.?
- Who would have access to the product?
- How could proprietary and public domain software be included?
- How could proprietary code be introduced into public domain?

7.4 Decision-support alternatives

As illustrated above, ecological risk management involves multiple participants. It also involves multiple domains (different stressors, different media, etc.) and multiple activities (data gathering, model development, analysis, etc.). Decision-support alternatives can be characterized along these 3 dimensions:

- audience — who uses the decision-support system?
- domain — what problem is it used on?
- scope — how is it used?

Different decision-support alternatives emphasize different dimensions. A few examples are provided below:

1) Broad domain, narrow audience and scope: A system designed to assist risk assessors by providing ready access to information on data and models for a broad range of problems. The system would have a limited audience (not stakeholders or risk managers) and scope (not analysis). This is primarily an informational system.

2) Broad scope, narrow audience and domain: A system designed to assist risk assessors by conducting a rapid screening analysis of a narrowly defined problem, e.g., evaluating a new chemical or a waste disposal site. This is primarily an analytical system.

3) Broad audience, narrow domain and scope: A system designed to assist stakeholders, risk managers, and assessors by guiding them through problem formulation; i.e., identification of the alternatives, the performance measures, and the key variables.

7.5 Potential development approaches

There were 3 potential development approaches discussed during the workshop, and these approaches are discussed below. Prior to the development of any conceptual approaches, the group discussed the important considerations relative to 2 contrary strategies of development. Strategy 1 was to rapidly develop a prototype that could be put out into the user community and subsequently upgraded in response to users' requests for modification. The second strategy was to establish a more elaborate development process and to design the system to match a problem-solving philosophy that matches the state-of-the-art for ERA. In the sections that follow, strategy 1 is explored in the form of the spreadsheet example, and strategy 2 is more closely aligned with the system example. Interestingly, a subgroup of the participants was able to identify an alternative prototype of the system example, which was named the data and model identification and acquisition system (DMIA) example. This later system focuses most heavily on supporting the front end of the problem-solving philosophy — problem formulation and model selection and acquisition. Additionally, the DMIA system would rely on the developing communications capability of the Internet to allow users to obtain the most current models.

7.5.1   Spreadsheet example

While the analogy may not be correct, the general ideas have merit. In this approach, one focuses the early development on producing as quickly as possible, a tool that provides a limited set of capabilities (focused on a limited set of problems) for the expert user. This tool would provide added value by speeding up or facilitating the expert's job or completing tasks that are difficult or arduous for the expert. Next, progressive addition of more tools to the expert's toolbox should occur at the same time the tool is being used by experts in the technical community. Through feedback from users, the development team produces macros that represent sets of activities an expert would perform regularly. This action supports both the expert and novice. From this point forward, the addition of new capabilities and the addition of simplifying macros proceeds as fast as possible to provide both a robust and a simple tool. This form of development is particularly appealing to commercial investors who are interested in early products that generate revenue as well as continued product release. On the other hand, this system does not, in general, base its steps of development on a problem-solving philosophy. Instead this is more suited to an "open toolbox" approach.

7.5.2   System example

There are several subsets of this approach in which the system is really based on a problem-solving philosophy. This requires a certain minimum level of capability in order for the user to understand that a system has been imposed on the process and to allow the user to carry out all the steps of the process in order to solve problems. The system example shares a common approach with the spreadsheet example in that it starts with a rudimentary set of capabilities and adds capabilities as development progresses through stages. The diagrams in Figure 7-3 show several potential arrangements of the system example. The following 5 types of system-based approaches are shown in Figure 7-3:

System platform 1—Library of tools (Plug-and-Play Model): In this approach a portion of the shell is built that houses the 3 universal capabilities of documentation, data access, and help text. Within the shell, the user can access various tools, but the order of use, type of use, and type of output are entirely unconstrained. In addition, the integration or linking of tools is not helped by the system.

System platform 2—Integrated toolkit (Antibody Model): In this approach, some of the links that facilitate moving information between components are well developed. Not all links are supported. Additionally, the process is not imposed on the user, who still has complete flexibility (no constraints). This step reduces the processing/analysis time, but does not provide consistency, etc.

System platform 3—Specific subset (Partial Pizza Model): In this approach, the entire computer system is contained in the shell. The user sees that any work is actually part of a bigger but somewhat constrained system. Only a subset of the steps of the process are supported. However, these pieces are thoroughly supported, much like they would be in the ultimate system.

System platform 4—(Geode or Clogged Artery Model): In this approach, the full system is present (all the steps are known and imposed on the user). However, instead of having a few thoroughly supported steps, all steps have some support, but are not capable of doing everything. In both of these 2 examples (3 & 4), the tools present for each step are linked for ease of access.

System platform 5—(Kaleidoscope Model): This is the ultimate system where all tools necessary to all problems are thoroughly linked and available. This is not a likely product.

While there are obviously other approaches, these examples provide some sense of what can be done. The next step is to address the following issues and define a development/funding strategy.

7.5.3   *Data and model identification and acquisition example*

Much of the effort expended at the workshop was directed at the earliest phases of an ERA. These phases include problem formulation and identifying appropriate models and data sources. Perhaps this is an indication that it is the earlier phases which consume most of the time spent on an actual assessment.

Problem formulation is crucial. This is a creative process, and it therefore requires attention and reasoning that is not readily provided by a computer. In contrast, searching libraries and computer files to identify and locate extant models, datasets, abstracts, and related risk assessments can be tedious, non-creative work. As such, the task is well-suited to computerization.

During the workshop, comparatively little attention was spent on the latter stages of the process, wherein the process yields an estimate of "risk" or "expected loss." Perhaps this indicates that actually running a selected model and interpreting the results are not such a great problem. Experience suggests that while this may be conceptually easy, in practice it can be quite labor-intensive. Therefore, careful selection of appropriate models or other quantitative methods early in the assessment process is important.

We suggest that a good first step towards the goal of assembling a comprehensive ERADSS would be to construct a system that would identify and/or retrieve relevant

1. Library of tools (Plug and Play Model)

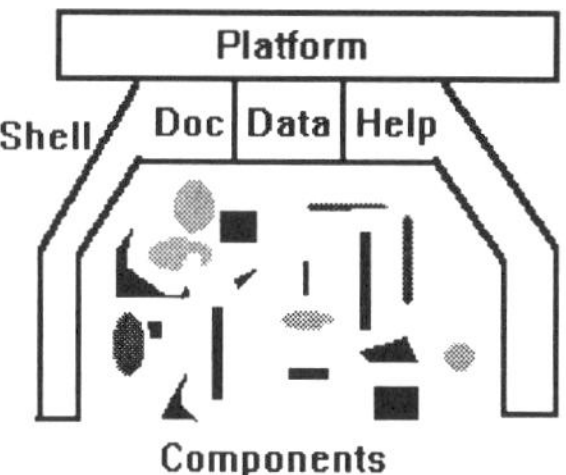

2. Integrated toolkit (Antibody Model)

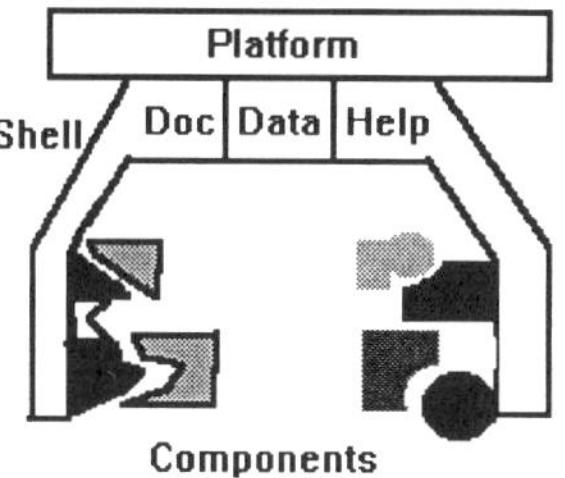

3. Specific subset (Partial Pizza Model)

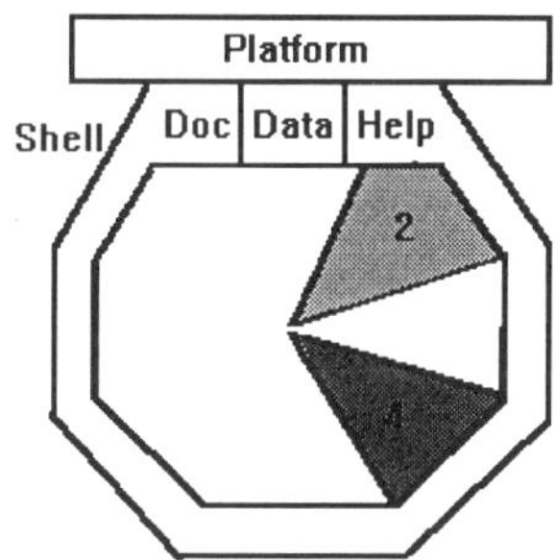

4. Geode (Clogged Artery Model)

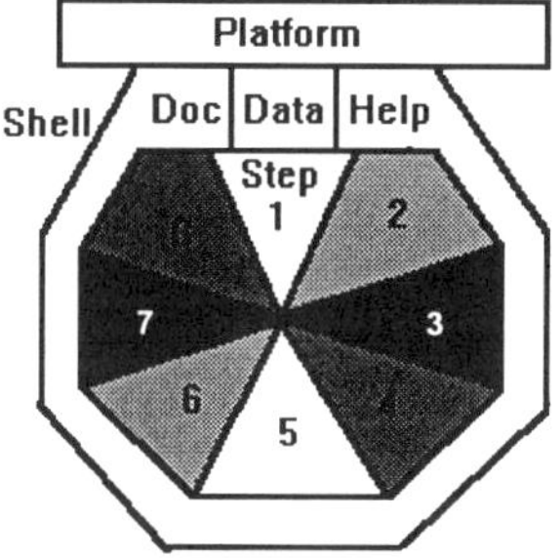

5. Kaleidoscope Model

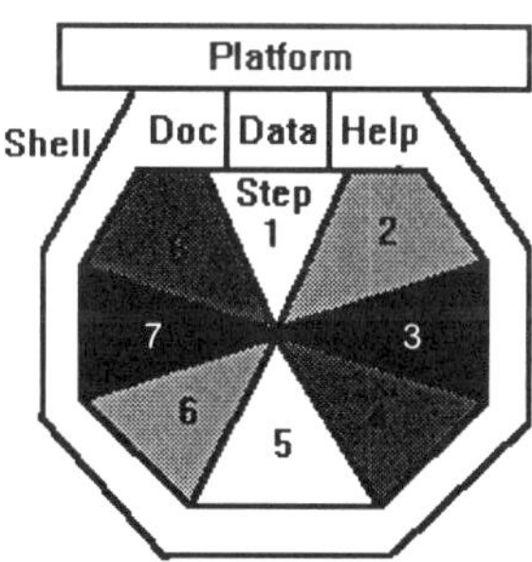

Figure 7-3   Potential system-based platforms or arrangements of the ERADSS

information. Because data are required for all of the other subsystems that have been described, it is clear that data acquisition would need to be done before any of the other systems could function. It should be possible to construct a useful DMIA system in a short time frame and at comparatively modest cost. Until a comprehensive system is completed, linking and using the data and/or models which are collected could be performed in a traditional manner. As the other components of the ERADSS are developing, the DMIA would be able to function independently and provide a useful service to the risk assessment community. It would also be able to support the ERADSS development process by providing information about existing databases, models, analysis protocols, and other related risk assessments that have been completed.

The DMIA would rely heavily on the expertise of users and their ability to formulate an appropriate question and to identify appropriate risk assessment strategies. The main function of the DMIA is to act like a research assistant provided with a well cross-referenced library card catalog: it accepts requests for information, provides limited feedback to clarify the request, collects information, and, finally, delivers information to the user with little or no interpretation attached to it (Figure 7-4). The user is then responsible for judging whether or not the information is useful and/or sufficient. The user is also left to act on the information, including making decisions on how to best use the information that was gathered.

The first version of the DMIA would be a simple marriage of existing programs that maintain and structure information (e.g., bibliographic databases) with those that perform network information dissemination, search, and retrieval. The core function of the DMIA would be to maintain a database that lists models, datasets and archives, authors, reports, abstracts, chemical protocols, and similar documentation relating to risk assessment. The major value-added aspects of the system would be the compilation of relevant titles and the creation and maintenance of the key descriptors for the listed items. For abstracts and reports, the key descriptors might be identical to the usual list of keywords.

For computer models, the descriptors would also include information about quality control/quality assurance checks, input/output features, operating platforms, cost and availability, and other information. Whenever possible, the DMIA would also maintain records of how a user can acquire the items in question. A slightly more advanced version of a DMIA would assist the user in actually downloading the information.

A more mature version of the DMIA could include features that might be termed "artificial intelligence" (AI) or "expert system." Artificial intelligence features of the system would operate during various phases of the process. For example, an AI feature would operate during the query structure phase. Here the system would serve to coach the user through the process of designing search criteria. Encoded risk assessment expertise would be used to help ensure that the task is sufficiently described. Artificial intelligence features would also operate in concert with the network search engines to help determine if a particular database contains relevant information. These operations would serve to

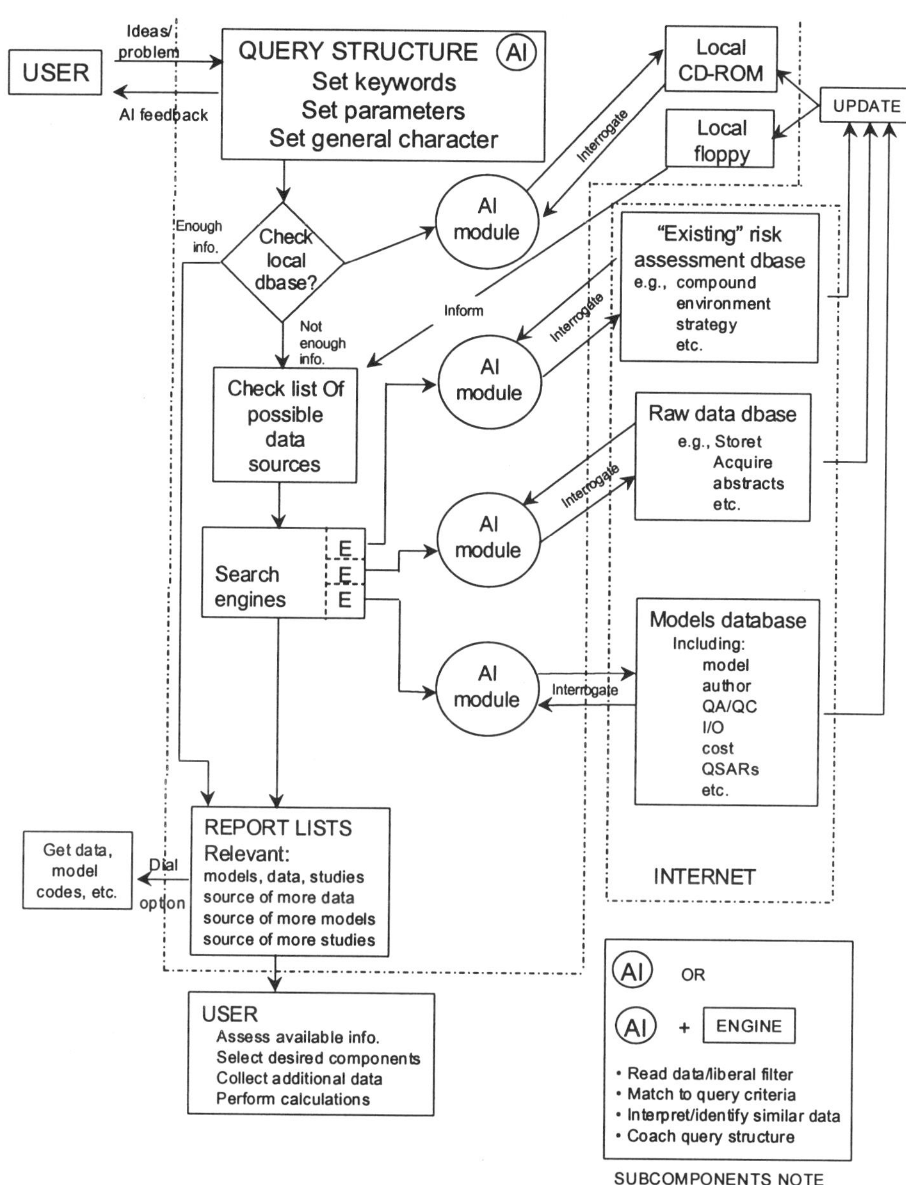

Figure 7-4   Data and model identification and acquisition (DMIA) decision-support system

construct an intelligent filter that would be able to make some judgments about whether a particular database (or a portion of it) is similar to the criteria set during the query structure phase. For example, this would be useful in a case where the user needs information on a particular molecule but would also be interested in records of related isomers. Records of the searching process would continuously update the DMIA's local records of database availability.

It is possible to construct a simple working version using elements of several existing programs by taking advantage of the existing Internet infrastructure. For example, an easily accessible, intuitive user interface could be constructed within the World Wide Web (WWW). The WWW is the successor to the popular Gopher hierarchical menu-driven system for distributing and accessing shared information. The WWW has many advantages over Gopher, including capability for formatted text, color, graphics, and multimedia. Easy-to-use interfaces can incorporate and integrate a number of other programs (Gopher, Telnet, and File Transfer Protocol) that enable a networked desktop Macintosh, personal computer, or Unix workstation both to access the WWW and to perform other functions. These interfaces can be tailored for particular platforms and are freely available for downloading from the WWW. While many professionals currently lack direct Internet access from their desktop, most probably have indirect access. Within a year or two, the majority will likely have direct access from their desktop.

A selected WWW server (of which thousands are available) would host a home page for the DMIA. Users would reach the home page in a variety of ways, including by direct access using a Uniform Resource Locator (URL) or via hypertext links on other WWW servers. Both the text on the home page and the text that would underlie it would contain hypertext links. These are created using HyperText Markup Language (HTML) commands to annotate plain ASCII text; this process can be carried out in any standard word processor. These links would provide point-and-click access to information about the DMIA and the information it has compiled. The search engine most appropriate for immediate use is Wide Area Information Servers (WAIS), developed for the Internet community by Thinking Machines, Inc. Versions of this are also in the public domain. Means of devising "intelligent agents" to search information on Internet is a current area of active research, results of which will support the AI features envisioned for the more mature version of the DMIA. Thus, common public-domain tools exist now to create a DMIA on the widely accessible WWW on the Internet.

The DMIA home page on the WWW would contain entries organized in an appropriate hierarchical structure for databases, models, protocols, reference books, existing risk assessments, and probably for other information categories not yet identified. These entries would be WAIS-indexed so that they could be easily searched. In addition, information would be provided on how to search other parts of the Internet for additional data and models. An audit mechanism would be used to capture information thus obtained so that the new information could be added to the DMIA system.

Software and an accepted infrastructure (the Internet) useful for creating a DMIA system already exist. Implementing a prototype system with these tools would be relatively fast and straightforward. Thinking needs to be done about the information (metadata) that should be collected about each database, model, or other entity to be included. Such metadata need to be able to support differentiation among the included materials in a useful and intuitive way so that users can readily locate relevant information while not having to sort through large amounts of irrelevant information. A part of the metadata would form a high-level hierarchy of organization of the information (for example, by type of media or class of endpoint).

A well-trained specialist (e.g., a graduate student in Library Science or Information Science) could provide useful assistance in the design of the system as well as in the design and initial collection of the metadata. Specialized types of programming expertise in coordination with experts in the field of ERA would be required to create the AI portions of the system.

7.6 Specific recommendations for developing a decision-support system

Specific components were identified by the risk-estimation workgroup for potential inclusion in a decision-support system:

- assessment of "drivers," including descriptions of types of risk assessments, time constraints, socio-economic considerations, etc. This component culminates in problem-formulation;
- decision analysis setup, including informal problem characterization, and expert consultation. This component leads to identification of assessment endpoints;
- endpoint development, including assembling a conceptual model, identification of measurement endpoints, and evaluation of endpoints;
- data and model review and assembly;
- assessment development, including identification of technical approaches, simulation modeling, data development;
- performance of the assessment;
- risk characterization; and
- sensitivity analysis and data worth.

Of these components, the development of the data and models review/assembly component merits development at this time as a potential prototype system. The DMIA approach proposed at the workshop could represent a contribution to ERA by facilitating directed data, model, and method identification. A system such as the DMIA appeared feasible and implementable at the time of the conference.

7.7   ERADSS development issues

The following issues represent some of the concepts, discussions, etc., that led to the development of the current process and list of potential supporting tools. Most of these issues are not fully resolved and are subjects of future workshops and/or discussion by the ERADSS software steering committee.

7.7.1   Data support

A number of risk-assessment framework modules rely upon accessing a large number of databases and GIS databases. While the framework does not exclude the existence of local databases, we do not assume that the databases accessed in a decision-support system will be housed at one site. The relevant data for many modules in the risk-assessment framework will likely be distributed across a number of sites. It is expected that each assessor cooperating in this project would collect and compile relevant data essential to the mission of the site, while making the databases available to other cooperating users. To this end, any implementation of the risk-assessment framework should consider using a structured query language (SQL)-compliant database management system (DBMS). Several SQL-compliant DBMSs exist under a number of operating systems. Both text-based and graphical query system products can access these DBMS systems though local area networks or across the Internet.

Implementation of a series of a distributed database allows the partitioning of responsibility of data collection and compilation among the user community. At the same time, it requires a high degree of cooperation and coordination among sites and users. Conversion of existing data collections to an SQL compliant DBMS would be critical to the success of a large scale implementation of the decision-support system, while local DBMSs would be sufficient for some partial implementations.

Quality assurance and documentation issues are critical to the successful use of the collected data with the general framework.

7.7.2   Module-to-module data interface

Many of the concepts set out in the risk-assessment process diagram depend on data and results from a program module being used as input into subsequent modules. While the transfer of data from one module to another can be done manually, it would be more satisfying if the transfer of data and results could be done automatically by the system. Many low level tools exist to accomplish this task, such as using Data Access Language (DAL), copying and retrieving information to the clipboard under System 7 or Windows, and graphical interfaces of UNIX. Software that contains a number of different software modules under one package generally handles these issues internally and is customized for each package. The development or implementation of a general tool to transfer information between risk-assessment modules or transfer data to the program shell has a number of desirable characteristics. These would include quicker response time, better use of project resources, and elimination of a source of typographical errors, as well as establishment of a consistent and documented approach to the management of modeling data between software modules integrated under one computer system. This software, once developed (with documentation), should be distributed at a very low cost to facilitate and promote usage.

We would suggest a future effort to determine the feasibility and resources required to develop a standardized data-interface software tool. This effort should include participants engaging in many aspects of the risk-assessment framework. The goal would be to establish written standards for data interfacing and determining the cost of the development.

7.7.3   *Estimated versus measured data*

A large-scale implementation of the decision-support system should accommodate estimated or measured input values or data. The strengths and limitations of using estimated values or field measurements were discussed from a limited perspective in relation to the case studies. Most ERAs are based on a combination of estimated and measured data.

7.7.4   *Sponsors and users*

In this section, prospective sponsors and users of the computer system products for ERA are considered. The intention is to identify the profiles of these groups and their corresponding needs with the hope that potential incentives or "drivers" to support the development and use of such products will surface.

Because they have different needs and interests, sponsors and users require separate consideration. However, there will be a significant overlap since most sponsoring organizations would likely include sponsors from the following categories

- government departments and agencies,
- industrial companies,
- research organizations,
- academic institutions,
- non-governmental organizations,
- consulting companies,
- investment institutions (e.g., development banks), and
- insurance companies.

Available funds for development will clearly depend on the number and type of sponsors obtained; equally, the desired capabilities of the product and therefore the required development budget will change depending on the number and type of sponsors. Some of the critical issues relating to sponsor groups are

- single versus multiple sponsorship,
- mix of government and non-government participants, and
- commercial interest in product development and sale.

Drivers or benefits, which are additional to the benefits of use of the products to be sponsored, must be identified. Otherwise, some prospective sponsors could decide to wait for others to develop the product. Sponsorship drivers may include

- decision-making involvement in product development process,
- sharing of experience and knowledge within sponsor group,
- shared cost of development between sponsors,
- peer pressure from similar organizations joining sponsor group,
- lower cost of use of products compared with non-sponsoring users, and
- priority/privileged treatment as a user.

Individuals who make the decision to sponsor may not be users, although they undoubtedly will take advice from prospective users within their organizations; they are more likely to be risk managers or more senior figures.

Users may be individuals with the following roles:

- risk managers or assessors,
- project engineers,
- operations engineers,
- site engineers, and
- central or corporate health safety or environmental experts.

The profile of a user was discussed extensively at the workshop. The most important distinction appears to be between a novice and an expert user. Individual users may emphasize different components of the ERA process. These users may have different priorities in the development of a decision-support system.

User benefits include the following:

- reduced direct costs for analysis and decision making;
- reduced indirect costs (e.g., liabilities, legal, regulatory, engineering, etc.), which may be potentially higher than direct cost savings;
- improved quality and utility of analysis;
- reduced cost of maintaining products
- transparency, reproducibility, and consistency improvements;
- increased productivity and efficiency of analysis;
- corporate memory to assist in reconstructing studies;

- enhanced training of risk assessors and managers; and
- improved access to databases and models.

7.7.5   *Cost-benefit analysis for system development*

The computer system development may be based on a cost-benefit analysis (CBA) approach (i.e., prioritization and selection of development options based on an evaluation of the costs and benefits of those options).

In order to facilitate a CBA approach to developing the system, an analysis of the ERA workload volume should be performed for the different principle applications:

- new product risks (FIFRA, TSCA),
- site environmental risk assessment (NEPA),
- remediation (RCRA, CERCLA, OPA),
- effluents (CWA, CAA),
- resource protection (endangered species, habitats), and
- business requirements (merger/acquisition, life-cycle assessment, eco-labeling, waste management).

The workload volume analysis should provide the following information:

- priority issues/applications on which to base marketing effort, (i.e., are there one or more applications which could support the development of the system?);
- identification of numbers and types of prospective users and sponsors;
- identification of specific functions required in ERA project work (information on regulations, study feasibility, problem-formulation, data gathering, model/data evaluation, processing data/models, and results manipulation); and
- potential costs of workloads and therefore cost savings due to computer system development.

Chapter 8

Discussion of workshop results

S. Bartell and G. Biddinger

Discussion of the decision-support system (DSS) focused on the overall scope of the system, the technical design of the system, methods for implementing the design, and possible technical and management implications of the existence of such a system. Major points addressing these issues are provided in the following text.

8.1   Feasibility and efficacy

Both the technical and operational feasibility of developing a DSS were major areas of exploration for the workshop participants. The lack of clarity on operational boundaries between risk assessors and risk managers, as perceived by the participants, made the discussions difficult. Issues related to feasibility are identified for both areas below.

8.1.1 Risk assessment

The workshop produced several alternative designs for a DSS for ecological risk assessment (ERA). The larger, comprehensive system would provide information, data, model access and integration, and computational capabilities for performing risk assessments in a probabilistic framework that is linked functionally to a separate DSS for risk management.

Workshop participants recognized that many of the component data systems, models, and tools (e.g., GIS, uncertainty methods, graphics, etc.) needed to perform ERAs are already available. The primary technical challenge lies in operationally connecting these components. Another technical challenge is identifying the specific datasets, models, and tools that would constitute the assessment portion of the overall system.

An alternative system could be developed that might be more easily assembled. The system would identify and facilitate access to data, models, and other tools that could contribute to assessing ecological risks in individual applications. However, this system would not operationally integrate data, models, and other tools to perform the assessment. The assessment would remain in the hands of the assessor. The major advantage to this system would be that as data, models, and computational methods are updated at their source, there would be no need to update the DSS, thereby avoiding rapid obsolescence and the need for version updates and distribution.

8.1.2 Risk management

The second area addressed concerned the risk-management phase of assessments. A major outcome of the workshop was the realization of the importance of the interface between risk assessment and risk management, as evidenced by follow-up discussions of the case studies and observing the problem-formulation activities in the case study role-playing or eco-risk theater (see Appendix B). The product of this risk-management phase of assessment overlaps and is important in helping to shape the problem-formulation phase of the current ERA framework. Workshop participants agreed that several risk-management or decision tools necessary to encode risk management activities are available. A similar challenge lies in integrating these tools in an overall system for risk assessment.

8.2 Decision-support tools: scope, boundaries, and system design

An important issue to the participants was the appropriate scope or boundary for the risk assessment decision-support system. Several participants supported limiting the scope of the system to only the actual risk characterization or risk estimation. Risk-management concerns and problem formulation would occur within this scope of the support system if such boundaries were followed. The system would essentially take the measurement endpoints as point of entry and bring the appropriate data, models, and other tools together to estimate risks. The integration of decision tools and problem-formulation actions might well take the form of an additional decision-support system; however, that system would be concretely separate and distinct from the assessment-support system. The product would be a system to assist risk assessors as the primary users.

An alternative concept included an operational system for the risk-management/problem-formulation phase of the assessment in addition to the tools necessary to estimate and characterize ecological risks. In fact, this comprehensive system placed more weight on encoding or capturing the management-formulation interactions than on the actual assessment. This system also emphasized the active and operational feedback between risk characterization and risk-based decision-making, including quantitative analysis of the worth of collecting new information in relation to the decision-making aspects of the overall assessment.

The workshop participants did not resolve the differences in scope demonstrated by the 2 alternatives, and other combinations and permutations of these 2 approaches were discussed as well. It was recognized that different examples of the mental models of the system might well emerge as tools of smaller scope in the future.

8.3 User community and application domain

One aspect of system design recognized as increasingly critical during the workshop was the determination of who might be the prime user of such a system. The expectations and capabilities of the user would certainly determine in large part the scope, components, and degrees of operational integration of the components. User requirements might also dictate the degrees of on-line help, coaching, and embedded constraints put into the support system. A truly generalized system would provide for detailed help and contain many menus with hypertext and tools for documentation of decisions made during an assessment. The expert user might choose to have all this available, but would want the flexibility to rapidly move through the system, particularly if the assessor addressed a similar problem (e.g., pesticide registration, new chemical manufacture) on a routine basis. Nonetheless, the documentation aspect of the system was recognized as valuable for both the novice and the experienced user.

Those participants with previous experience in the design and implementation of the kind of system envisioned here suggested that the ERA system should be designed with an expert user in mind.

8.4 Implementation of a decision-support system

Several alternative mechanisms for implementation of a decision-support system were examined and discussed in different levels of detail.

8.4.1 Government institutions

Several participants offered the opinion that only a large government institution could command the resources necessary to develop the larger comprehensive risk-management/risk-assessment system. Importantly, it was recognized that government support might be international in scope. The risk- assessment system might serve to help harmonize efforts to standardize assessment protocols on an international scale. Organizations such as the Organization for Economic Cooperation and Development might be important supporters and contributors to the development and implementation of the system.

8.4.2 Neutral foundations

A neutral organization or foundation might be put in place to facilitate the development and implementation of the risk-assessment system. For example, the SETAC Foundation for Environmental Education might serve in this role. The Foundation would assist in acquiring, sustaining, and managing the necessary financial resources to construct the system. The organization could also provide necessary maintenance and updates once the prototype was assembled and in use. The Foundation or other neutral organization could also work to market the system.

8.4.3 Private sector involvement

Workshop participants also recognized that the private sector could serve as a rapid and efficient mechanism for developing and marketing the ecological risk assessment decision-support system (ERADSS). However, it appears more likely that the private sector would develop smaller systems with limited scope (e.g., rapid systems to perform screening calculations) to test the market and economy of such ventures. If a product proved economically viable, the producer might construct future versions with additional, more advanced risk-assessment capabilities, in much the same way that word processors, spreadsheets, and so forth have developed over the past decade. One interesting workshop observation was that the first product on the market might dominate the course of future product development by its very existence, independent of the quality of the product. Several smaller businesses might work together to produce the larger more comprehensive system.

8.4.4 Self-organization

One innovative suggestion was to "seed" computer networks (e.g., the Internet) with opportunities for any interested party on the network to participate in the development of the ERADSS. As a result of investigators working alone or in collaboration using global computer networks, the ERA system might in essence organize itself. The role of a neutral foundation might then be to serve as the monitor and custodian of the Internet home of the support system. Of course, this approach is more complex than suggested by these brief words; such an approach might provide for a massive and continually evolving response from a diverse set of contributors and potential users.

8.5 Efficacy of the decision-support system for ecological risk assessment

The preceding discussion of the workshop reflected the opinion that constructing such a system is a worthwhile endeavor to be supported by the ERA community at large. Several aspects supporting this opinion and its opposite were discussed at the workshop.

8.5.1 Supporting viewpoints

Several points argue for the development and implementation of a system. First, the existence and use of a system would bring additional attention to providing for improvements and consistency in ERA. This issue underscores current activities (e.g., U.S. Environmental Protection Agency, National Research Council, Water Environment Research Foundation) to develop common methods and approaches for performing ERAs. Second, the development of such a system could force meaningful considerations concerning the degrees to which ERA can be standardized, given that such activities are currently underway (e.g., American Society for Testing and Materials). Finally, the existence of such a system would provide a focus, even if it is a controversial one, for advancing the science of ERA.

8.5.2 Opposing viewpoints

The majority of workshop participants supported the advancement towards implementation of the comprehensive DSS. However, several reasons were offered, often vigorously, why this system was a dangerous idea. For one, such a system was seen as an eventual impediment to the advancement of the science. Once in place, with an institutional and marketing life of its own, the system might prove highly resistant to change and improvement. Should the system become the DSS through the aegis of some regulatory agency, innovations and scientific advancements might be for naught until they received agency approval. As a result, new capabilities in ERA might develop at a pace dictated by the regulators, not scientists. Similarly, if such a system were adopted, it might gain legal precedent merely through its use. Other methods of assessment, while perhaps just as technically valid, might not gain legal standing simply because those systems were not used to perform the assessment. Finally, the existence of the system, particularly if in the private sector, might unduly influence the direction of future developments in ERA because any innovation would have to be compatible with the prevailing system.

The workshop participants differed in opinion as to whether such concerns were sufficient to prohibit the future exploration and development of the DSS. Several people agreed that the decision was no longer that of the workshop participants, who represent only a small sample of those who might actually develop and/or use such a system in the future.

8.6   Future development and implementation

In the concluding general plenary session, the workshop participants discussed the implementation strategy for developing a DSS for ERA. Key steps in the development process are outlined below.

1) *Produce a document that generally describes the system for peer review, user focus surveys, and discussions with potential funders.*

    The participants suggested that the system design developed during the workshop should be communicated broadly to assess the interest of the user community and their feedback on first steps. A number of techniques were suggested as mechanisms to accomplish the communication. A 4-page scoping document was recommended as the basis of SETAC newsletter articles and for discussion at open forums. The summary could be the basis for dialogues with peer groups and more focused discussions with potential users and funding organizations.

    An additional suggestion was to put the conceptual design of the system on the Internet to solicit a wide range of opinion, review, and contributions to the project.

2) *Establish a software development steering group under the auspices of the SETAC Ecological Risk Assessment Advisory Group to explore approaches to funding, managing, maintaining, and updating a DSS.*

    Initially, the responsibility of communicating workshop documentation would be the responsibility of the workshop steering committee. Subsequently, if interest is sufficient to proceed with the development of a system, a new steering committee for the system needs to be set up. A first step for this group would be the design of a prototype system that can be discussed in user focus groups. Also, it was suggested that a computer-based simulation of the prototype would be a useful aid in these focus discussions.

3) *Define a limited prototype system that could be available in less than 2 years.*

The group felt that this recommendation was appropriate if the initial system was developed for an expert user. The system should be focused on helping the expert formulate the problem and gain access to data and models. In the first version, the datasets and models would be accessed from outside the system. The system should remain flexible so that advances in the sciences used in risk assessment could be addressed in the use of the system in the future. An example of this prototype is the DMIA discussed in Chapter 7 (Figure 7-3).

4) *Recommend the SETAC Foundation for Environmental Education as a neutral organization for administrating funds.*

Funding would likely be needed from a consortium of government and private industry. Participants did not see that the development costs would likely be born by a small software company and that the user community would have to support that development. The group felt that because of SETAC's nonprofit status in the U.S., SETAC could act as the coordinator of contributions from a diverse group of organizations and as manager for the prototype development.

Update to workshop

At the August 1994 Pellston workshop, the lively discussions of concepts, issues, methods, and technologies that addressed the feasibility and structure of a decision-support system for ecological risk assessment appeared timely, perhaps even somewhat futuristic. The workshop operated (at least implicitly) under the proposition that ecological risk assessment had reached a stage of scientific maturity that permitted standardization, and importantly, that computerizing any standard approach was a worthwhile objective. To some workshop participants, the notion of usefully capturing the process of ecological risk assessment in an integrated hardware-software package may have seemed at best ill-advised, at worst, simply preposterous. To their credit, the participants at Pellston seriously applied themselves to the workshop objectives and laid aside their preconceptions. Importantly, a conceptual prototype of a decision-support system for assessing ecological risks emerged as the result of spirited debate, welcome disagreements, and hard-won consensus.

Much has happened since the 1994 workshop. The development and standardization of the process of ecological risk assessment in North America was just beginning at that time and will likely continue in earnest at least under the auspices of the USEPA (e.g., USEPA 1996), the Society of Environmental Toxicology and Chemistry, and the American Society for Testing and Materials (e.g., ASTM Committee E 47) and through industry-led efforts (e.g., American Industrial Health Council, Chemical Manufacturers Association, American Crop Protection Association, and the American Petroleum Institute). Efforts aimed at developing and standardizing methods and approaches for assessing ecological risks are also well underway worldwide in the European Union, the Netherlands, Japan, and throughout the Organization for Economic Cooperation and Development (OECD). Such developments are occurring in both the public and private sector. Interestingly, many of the advantages and disadvantages of standardizing the risk assessment process, debated earlier at the Pellston conference and presented in this volume, remain key topics of discussion in more recent and continuing efforts in refining, modifying, and embellishing the enterprise of ecological risk assessment.

Since the 1994 Pellston workshop, there have been several attempts to construct decision-support systems for assessing ecological risks. These ventures have been undertaken by both public and private sector entities. At Pellston, we discussed the advantages and disadvantages of identifying an organizational focal point for developing ecological risk assessment decision-support systems. In the absence of such an institution, individuals and companies have developed automated risk assessment capabilities largely on their own. These systems range in complexity from an automated process for selecting from available USEPA environmental transport-and-fate models (i.e., USEPA - Integrated

Model Evaluation System, IMES) to more comprehensive decision-support systems for estimating and reporting risks, for example, related to groundwater contamination (e.g., Sandia Environmental Decision-Support System, SEDDS). Also, ecological effects models are being integrated with decision support software. Thus, despite legitimate concerns expressed at Pellston regarding the difficulties in developing these kinds of systems, decision-support systems for assessing ecological risks are in fact being constructed, and more importantly, used.

Progress toward materially realizing the kinds of systems developed only in concept at Pellston has been abetted in no small way by the continuing advances and increased availability of inexpensive computational power and highly interactive software development tools. The proliferation of data, information, and software available electronically (i.e., the Internet) has also fostered a technical and methodological environment conducive to the development of an integrated risk assessment system. As anticipated at the workshop, likely technical roadblocks to the eventual development of a decision-support system for ecological risk assessment would result from limitations, not in hardware and software, but in institutional commitment, personal resolve, and "gray ware." Continued progress in removing these roadblocks has been evident since the earlier deliberations at Pellston represented in this volume.

The Pellston workshop organizers and participants look forward to future innovations in the development and application of decision-support systems for assessing ecological risks. It is hoped that all of the optimistic prognostications regarding the efficacy of such decision tools will be borne out in the years to come, while the many concerns expressed about such an ambitious undertaking are at the same time laid to rest.

Steve Bartell
Kevin Reinert
Greg Biddinger

March 1998

List of participants

The affiliations and addresses of the steering committee and the participants are shown as they were in 1994. These affiliations may have changed, but as the participants' organizations supported them, the workshop, and the development of these proceedings, this in some minor way provides them with some recognition.

Ecological risk assessment modeling system steering committee

Kevin Reinert
Rohm and Haas Company
Toxicology Department
Spring House, PA

Steve Bartell
SENES Oak Ridge, Inc.
Center for Risk Analysis
Oak Ridge, TN

Lawrence Burns
USEPA ERL
Athens, GA

Peter deFur
Environmental Defense Fund
Washington, DC

Jack Gentile
USEPA ERL
Narragansett, RI

Dwayne Moore
Commercial Chemicals
Evaluations Branch
Environment Canada
Hull, Quebec Canada

Gerald Niemi
University of Minnesota
Natural Resources Research
Duluth, MN

Robert Goldstein
Environmental Science
Electric Power Research
Institute
Palo Alto, CA

Ecological risk assessment advisory group

Gregory Biddinger
ERAAG Chair
Exxon Biomedicine
Sciences, Inc.
East Millstone, NJ

Rodney Parrish
Executive Director
SETAC
Pensacola, FL

Gregory Schiefer
Associate Exec. Director
SETAC
Pensacola, FL

Ecological risk assessment modeling system workshop participants

Adam Borison
Applied Decision Analysis
Menlo Park, CA

Steven Bradbury*
USEPA Environmental Research
Laboratory
Duluth, MN

David Cacela
RCG/Hagler Bailly, Inc.
Boulder, CO

Carl Chen
Systech Engineering
San Ramon, CA

Sigurd Christensen
Environmental Sciences Division
Oak Ridge National Laboratory
Oak Ridge, TN

Christina Cowan
The Procter & Gamble Company
Environmental Science Department
Cincinnati, OH

Mark Evans
Agency for Toxic Substance &
Disease Registry
Atlanta, GA

David Gess
Decision Focus, Inc.
Mountain View, CA

Lev Ginzburg
Applied Biomathematics
Setauket, NY

Joop Hermens
University of Utrecht
RITOX
Utrecht
The Netherlands

Robert Hunter
University of Minnesota
Duluth, MN

John Irwin
USEPA
OAQPS
Research Triangle Park, NC

Michael Johnson
Center for Environ. & Water
Resources Engineering
University of California
Davis, CA

Huw Jones
DNV Industry UK
DNV Technica Ltd.
London, England

Paul Kaplan
Sandia National Laboratory
Albuquerque, NM

Walter Karcher
European Chemicals Bureau
European Commission
JRC Ispra Environment Institute
Ispra, Italy

Joshua Lipton*
RCG/Hagler Bailly, Inc.
Boulder, CO

Thomas Natan
Hampshire Research Institute
Alexandria, VA

Brock Neely
EnviroSafe Inc.
Midland, MI

Benjamin Parkhurst*
The Cadmus Group, Inc.
Laramie, WY

Rich Purdy
3M Environmental Engineering
and Pollution Control
St. Paul, MN

Carl Richards
University of Minnesota
Duluth, MN

Keith Solomon
Center for Toxicology
University of Guelph
Guelph, Ontario, Canada

Cees van Leeuwen*
Directorate General for
Environmental Protection
Bilthoven
The Netherlands

Akula Venkatram*
University of California-Riverside
Riverside, CA

Erik Webb*
Sandia National Laboratory
Albuquerque, NM

Douglas Winkelmann
Exxon Biomedical Sciences, Inc.
East Millstone, NJ

* Group chairs

Description of and insights from case studies

Three case studies were developed by the steering committee. The case studies were utilized as the basis for a workshop exercise that could be described as a bit of eco-risk theater. Participants in the workshop were divided into "operational units" which represented stages of the ecological risk assessment (ERA) process. The flow of information from the risk manager to the assessor to operational units and back again were mapped by a group of computing system experts. The purpose of these exercises was to get an operating pattern that could be used as the basis for the design of a decision-support system. The group was charged with using a preliminary risk assessment decision model developed during the workshop to define the problem and carry out an assessment.

Case study assumptions

The following assumptions were used:

- the groups would use the existing system presented by the system-design group as an accurate representation of the process thus far;
- no additional input or modification to the scheme was considered necessary to start/complete the exercise;
- the groups would function as a team, taking individual steps/actions en masse (e.g., we would not play roles);
- the group identified recorders and charged the systems design representative with keeping the process on track; and
- the focus was on the process rather than on some other diversion.

After working through 3 case studies and discussing the strengths and weaknesses of the risk assessment process, each of the 5 component groups met separately to address the following questions concerning a potential modeling/decision-support system. 1) What are the strengths and weaknesses of the system for your component group with respect to the 3 case studies? 2) How will the component fit within the overall system? 3) What is the state of science with respect to your component? 4) Where are the evident data or knowledge gaps, and how might those gaps be resolved? 5) What are the suggested future steps with regard to your component and the potential modeling system under consideration? As expected, because of a) the disparate nature of the components, b) the differences in degree of understanding among the components, and c) the mix of personalities and expertise among members of the groups, each of the summaries has its own flavor and degree of resolution on the questions posed.

Summary

In general, each of the component groups identified many strengths and weaknesses that would be inherent in any ERA system. For example, the fate-and-effects group emphasized the importance of stating the risk assessment in terms of a testable hypothesis, while the model-testing and evaluation group focused on the importance of quantifying uncertainty in ecological risk models. Most groups especially illustrated how the weaknesses could lead to substantial problems and misinterpretations in the risk assessment results.

Each of the component groups also briefly summarized the state of the science for their respective area. Again, there was considerable variability in responses depending on the component group and the degree to which the discipline has evolved. For example, since data have been gathered for long periods of time, the data group emphasized the varying degrees in availability of information. Databases have been relatively well-developed for toxic effects data, but are almost non-existent for higher levels of biological organization, such as communities or ecosystems. In contrast, the risk- estimation group summarized many approaches to predictive risk estimation, but noted how infrequently these methods are applied in real world settings.

Most of the component groups also identified where the largest gaps exist and how these gaps may be resolved in the future. Many of these gaps will not be easily resolved because of limitations in monetary resources, lack of understanding among scientists, regulators, and the public, and the absence of standardization in the ecological risk assessment process.

An underlying theme within these component reports and throughout the workshop was that the components of ERA are in a dynamic, evolving state of scientific complexity. Hence, any potential system development must recognize this state and stimulate advancement of capabilities in assessing ecological risk.

Summaries of the case study details as presented to the workshop participants and any attempt to capture some of the dynamic interactions and responses of the participants to the exercise follows. One of the most dramatic learnings was the lack of iterative interaction between the risk assessor and the risk manager. This issue subsequently was addressed in an editorial by Moore and Biddinger (1995) who called for better definition of the dialogue between risk assessors and their risk managers.

Case study learnings

General learnings from the risk assessor/risk manager teams during the eco-risk theater were captured. Observations and learnings from each of the risk assessor/risk manager teams were pooled from the 3 case studies and are presented below.

1) During the problem-formulation phase, the process of determining assessment endpoints after receiving the charge from the risk manager was chaotic and not at all transparent. The decisions made at this initial stage of the process have a dramatic and deterministic effect on the assessment and the utility of the assessment

to the risk manager. Several system design questions resulted from the discussion. This point may suggest or require inclusion of a decision-support system at the initial stage of problem formulation. The initial stage probably should include a coach system that guides the user through a series of steps to be taken, but does not actually carry out an analysis. This initial stage of problem formulation occurs in consultation with parties such as stakeholders, who must be designated outside the expert system or within it. The last point was considered essential in terms of system content and design.

2) Key assessment endpoints were not selected during the problem-formulation stage in these cases. Several system design issues resulted. The assessor and/or the manager must have sufficient knowledge of the facts, the system, and the data before entering the problem-formulation stage of an expert system. In real cases, the problem-formulation stage is an iterative process often involving many types of experts and information. The cases used the expertise of fate-and-effects modelers, data managers and modelers, risk assessors, and risk managers. The iteration resolved the following questions:

   - Will the assessment be useful?
   - What is the probabilistic nature of the endpoint under consideration?
   - What should the assessment measure?
   - What data and models are available?

3) In the cases as played, little consideration was given as to how uncertainty would be carried through the system. Rather, it was given only narrow consideration in isolation. System design must account for uncertainty in some fashion. Many on-line databases available to most risk assessors at present do not have information on variance and uncertainty. This weakness has to be treated in some way, either by access to the original literature or some other means. Furthermore, dose-response relationships that are necessary for making certain determinations are not stored in on-line databases. Either these data must be provided some other way, or the system must operate around them. Coaching cues may be useful or necessary in requiring uncertainty analysis during, rather than at the end of, the process.

4) The role of the model-testing and evaluation team was unclear. The system-design group should consider how to correct this operational deficiency. Specifically, the role of this group may be more in the construction and updating (maintenance) of the expert system beforehand, rather than involvement in individual cases.

5) As the cases proceeded, secondary and derivative questions arose from the initial risk estimation, prompting new, related assessment endpoints. A number of options exist to deal with this feature of the way problems are solved in assessment. The system could be set up as a sequential system by design, as an option or in some other fashion. The risk manager has an important role to play in the formulation and delineation of these derivative questions. The risk manager must determine if and when these questions need to be answered.

6) None of the case studies in the first round provided a realistic simulation of the process of ERA as practiced by any of the members of the group. The participants made a number of observations on this point. The sequencing of the groups was unusual and did not necessarily follow patterns used in real practice. The cases did not access the data as much as the data occur in a real process; in reality, data enter into the process at every point and during iterative stages as well. The process did not involve, nor did it require, any hypothesis development. The system design group was cautioned not to rely on the case studies as representative of the real world process in creating a template for an expert-support system.

7) The case studies provided a range of ERA types and problems. The endpoints, assessment goals, data requirements, and scales (temporal and spatial) varied greatly by design of the conference organizers. The conference attendees asked if a single expert system was amenable for application to such disparate cases.

8) The observers raised the question of the role of risk management and risk managers in the system. In these initial cases studies, neither the risk manager nor risk management had a clearly defined position in the process.

Case study I - 1,1,1-trichloroethane

Problem formulation

The primary question that needs to be addressed is that given that 1,1,1-trichloroethane (TCA) is on the Montreal Protocol and will be phased out of production within 2 years, should there be control measures to remove it from production/use sooner? To answer this question there are 3 subsidiary questions that need to addressed: 1) What will be the environmental costs if we continue to use TCA for more than 2 years? 2) What will be the economic costs of earlier phase-out? 3) What will be the costs and ecological risks of replacements for TCA? This later question is included because we did not want to phase out TCA and replace it with an alternative compound that is worse.

General comments on the system

The ecological risk assessment decision-support system (ERADSS) suggests entry into the system at the "type of assessment" box (see Table B-1). We could conceivably use the system, especially data access and maybe screening level models, to identify assessment and measurement endpoints. For this case study, we suggest that entry to the system be at the "point of informal characterization of problem" or "endpoint identification" box.

Guidance documents and directives from the European Union, the Organization for Economic Cooperation and Development, etc., can be used to define the details of the assessment process including the assessment steps and definition and format of initial basic data and subsequent datasets. These next steps often provide incremental refinements to defined screening methods which can be examined to decide which steps are most cost effective to implement.

The normal risk assessment approach is to compile, sort, and screen all measurement endpoints initially, then decide on which ones to focus on for subsequent refinement (data collection, re-analysis) and to identify alternative endpoints.

Table B-1 *Summary of the strengths and limits of the process as identified in Case Study 1*

System/assessment component	Strengths	Limitations
Problem definition/endpoint selection	Basing pathway through system on assessment type is probably a good idea.	Need for some data before selecting endpoints (e.g., release data, media int which released, geographic scale and patchiness of use/release, temporal scale, physical/chemical data, known acute or chronic effects of the chemical) Screening level multi-media model (to identify media for consideration in identifying possible endpoints).
Reviewing existing data	If there are places where data are available and if these data are easily queried and compiled, this could be very beneficial. Uncertainty of data also useful	QSARs need to have domains of use, reliability, documentation, source assumptions, etc. identified. (Guidance document for using QSARs in chemical risk assessment will be available shortly.) Text required to help assessor learn to judge quality of measured or raw data.
Modeling fate/effects		Need to add flow chart of model testing and validation to this task. No performance statistics needed for screening level model. Screening methods should be constructed so as to provide suggestions for next steps to incrementally refine the screening method.
Risk characterization	Recognizes need for different risk estimators	Need to add direct interaction of modeling and risk characterization (This involves running additional cases.)
Sensitivity analysis and data worth/cost analysis	Gives relationship between data and results to identify most cost-effective way to proceed to more data collection.	If screening test fails, cannot assess value of refining data because no probabilities are used for screening test
Data collection		Need to indicate that either effects or fate data or both can be refined.

Potential user groups for system

The following groups are potential users for the system:
- chemical companies for assessing new substances,
- insurance companies considering liability for sites and chemical releases,
- site characterization and assessment for small- to medium-sized sites, and

- regulatory agencies: federal, regional, state, and local.

Assessing the procedure with TCA

In this exercise, an initial screen using the unit world fugacity model (Mackay and Paterson 1982) was used to estimate the likely distribution of TCA in the ecosystem (Figure B-1). Input to the model was obtained from the simple physical and chemical properties of TCA (vapor pressure, water solubility, log K_{ow}, and Henry's

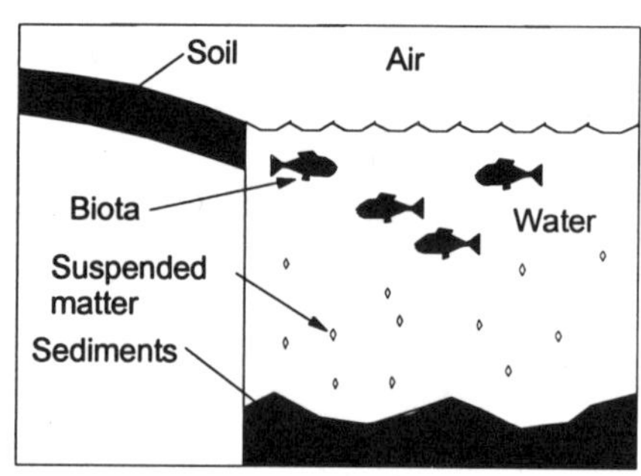

Figure B-1   Model environment for fugacity level 1 calculations

Law constant). The result of this modeling exercise suggested that the majority of the TCA would be distributed in the air with some in the water. This was confirmed by consulting databases for atmospheric analyses and analyses of water at water purification plants. It was recognized that TCA could enter groundwater through spills and that concentrations in these instances may be high. However, the movement of TCA into surface waters would likely be so slow that concentrations would not be raised significantly. The risks were judged to be highest to terrestrial organisms and aquatic organisms to a lesser extent.

Expressing the results of a refined risk-characterization analysis as a distribution of toxicity values rather than a single point estimate is an approach presently being used by the Dutch government (Health Council of the Netherlands 1993). A major advantage of this approach is that it uses all relevant single species toxicity data, and when combined with exposure distributions, allows quantitative estimations of risks to aquatic organisms. An illustration of the principle is shown in Figure B-2, adapted from Cardwell et al. (1993). This approach is based on several assumptions: 1) it is assumed that the distribution of acute susceptibility represents the "universe" of species and is log-normal with respect to concentration (shown as a cumulative frequency distribution in Figure B-2) and 2) it is also assumed that the chronic toxicity of a compound is log-normally distributed.

The degree of overlap of the exposure curve with the effects curve can be used to estimate the probability that a certain percentage of aquatic species may be adversely affected. There are several outcomes of this approach. The distribution of EEC-1 has little overlap with the chronic toxicity distribution, suggesting that there will be little impact from this situation. The distribution of EEC-2 is such that more overlap is present. In this situation, it is likely that chronic effects will be observed unless mitigation measures can move the EEC distribution to the left or increase the steepness of the slope. This could be done by identifying those environmental situations that lead to the high EECs or those very sensitive species and restricting the use of the product to environments or areas where the sensitive species do not occur. In the case of EEC-3, chronic effects will likely be observed in almost all instances, and major mitigation steps may be required. In the Dutch sys-

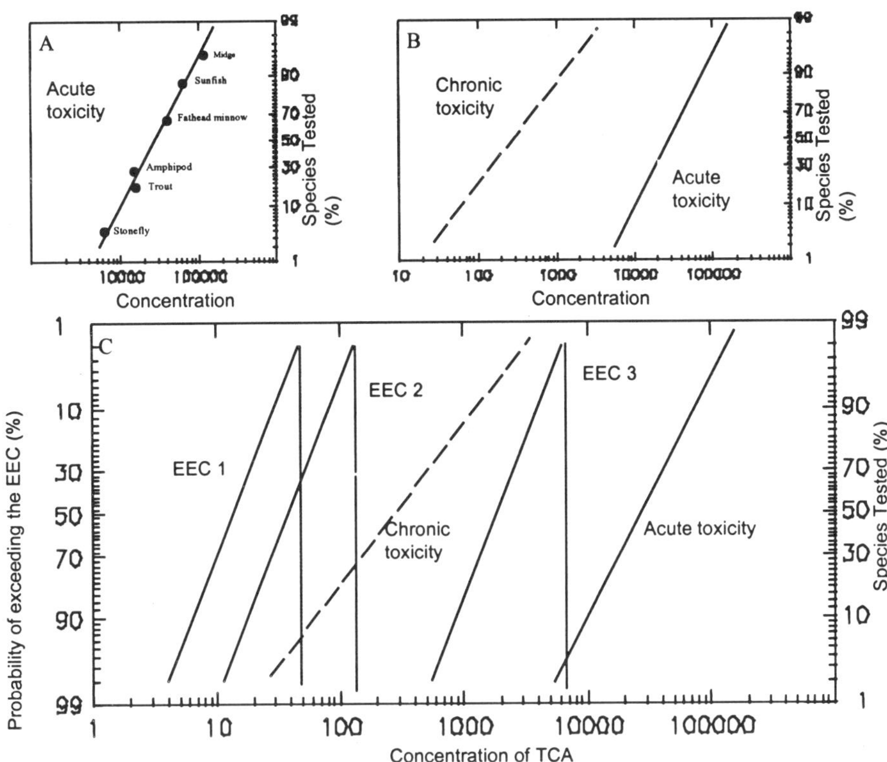

Figure B-2   Comparison of expected environmental concentrations (EEC) for a substance with concentrations causing acute and chronic toxicity

tem, major distributions of chronic toxic effects (no observed effect concentrations [NOECs]) are used to estimate the concentration of a chemical at which only 5% of the species would be affected. In other words, at the chosen level of protection, there is a chance that 5% of the aquatic species may be affected. In using overlaps of distributions, there is a tacit assumption that protecting a certain percentage of species for a certain proportion of occasions will also preserve ecosystem structure and function. Given the natural variability between sites within ecosystems and even between ecosystems, this assumption will probably hold. However, this is a controversial area and more research will be needed.

There are some limitations to this approach. For example, the choice of protection level (e.g., 90% of species) may not be socially acceptable. Some may view 90% as being over-protective, while others may find that level of risk unacceptable, especially if the 10% of potentially affected species includes organisms of high ecological, commercial, or recreational significance. In addition, risks of persistent, bioaccumulative chemicals to species at the top of the food chain may not be sufficiently considered by this approach alone. In the former situation, these species could be identified and appropriate mitigation measures taken.

An attempt was made to conduct a probabilistic assessment of risk for TCA. In this case, good environmental concentration data were available. Less toxicity data were available but knowledge of the fact that TCA is a narcotic sug-

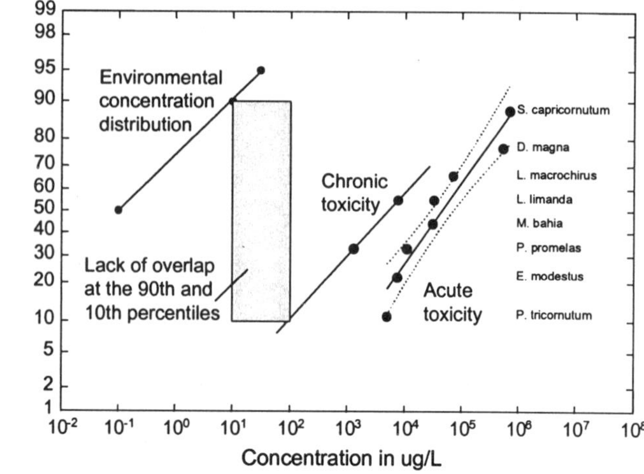

Figure B-3   Probabilistic risk assessment of TCA for aquatic organisms

gested that toxicity to the "universe of organisms" would likely span a relatively narrow range of about 1000 (J. Hermens, personal communication). The results of this are shown in Figure B-3.

The large margin between the range of concentrations found in the Canadian aquatic environment and the sensitivity range suggests that TCA does not represent a risk to aquatic organisms. This case study did not address terrestrial organisms as receptors or, more importantly, potential ozone depletion by TCA.

Case study II - Commencement Bay

Case information

Using the Commencement Bay issue paper (USEPA 1993) as a basis, we abstracted/extracted a core of information on physical, chemical, and biological measurements made by a state agency as part of some field study process. These data consisted of the following:

- samples of surface water and sediment around the bay, including references, were screened for 150 chemicals;
- the sampling sites contained some or all of the following toxic substances: phenol, PAHs, PCBs, TCDFs, 4-methylphenol, 1,4-dichlorobenzene, 8 metals;
- the above chemicals were higher at the sampling sites than at the reference sites;
- PCBs were detected in muscle and liver of English sole;
- metabolites of PAHs were found in fish and crabs;
- fish with skin and liver tumors were collected in the bay; and
- benthic communities in tideflats had changed from reference sites in the region.

Information about the site includes the following:
- site is a heavily industrialized area,
- tideflats were formed at the mouth of the river delta,
- the bay is relatively shallow (<60 ft),
- commercial harvesting of bivalves is prohibited,
- 4 species of salmon are harvested commercially and recreationally in the bay,
- the benthos consists of 407 species, but a few tolerant polychaetes and bivalves dominate,
- 7 species of flatfish occur in the bay, and
- the bay is a migratory pathway for anadromous fish and for waterfowl.

The state raised the initial problem to a city (or other local) elected official in a sufficiently (or explicitly) public fashion to attract the attention of the public. The next step was a call to action and an alert by the local public official to deal with the issue. The public official had numerical data in the form of a report from the state and came to the assessment team for help. The public official was responsible for answering the public concern and is the party who convened the risk assessment team. The public official was thus termed the risk manager and served this function.

The risk assessment team formed and acted via deliberation as a single entity. No other roles were assigned, and the group operated by agreement. The case manager assumed the position of risk manager when needed. The group moved to formulate the problem via question formulation, hypothesis statement, etc.

The system design group quickly asked the case study group to return to the previous step—scoping or pre-problem formulation. This step was the one that set the context for not only the risk assessment team, but also, as importantly, for the risk manager. This group included the stakeholders and pertinent advisory parties. At this stage, a fair amount of discussion focused on the roles of the initial stages and the tasks to be performed. Consultation between the risk manager and the stakeholder group was accepted as the first step, prior to the risk assessment. The group did not agree under which step the stakeholder consultation should be included. The general opinion was that it was a risk management step.

The group agreed that a management element enters into the system at the first stage. The issue is that the risk management/risk assessment team formulates the problem in the context of the situation in which the concern was raised. Therefore, the concern of the stakeholders must form the basis for the assessment endpoint. The group then restarted with the context setting stage at or prior to the problem formulation. From this step came the identified concern that there were 2 issues for the case: the immediate public health threat of contaminated fish, and the larger one of whether the environmental problem was serious (i.e., is the ecosystem threatened?). These took the form of the following:

1) Are the fish safe to eat? The assessment team used this question as a first tier, recognizing that human health threats often precede ecological ones in a public context. The issue directly addressed the concerns of the stakeholder group, rather than the concerns of the risk assessment team, even if the two differ.

2) Is the ecosystem harmed by this contamination?

The risk assessment team and the risk manager discussed the question back and forth, and the team consulted without the risk manager. Both levels of consultation were efforts to refine the questions, specifically the information needed, and to determine the scope of the project. Iteration continued until the assessment team was satisfied that the risk manager knew what was wanted and what would be delivered. The risk manager then checked with the stakeholder committee.

The results of the problem identification/formulation step were agreement to rapidly make 2 determinations, sequentially, on different schedules: quickly answer the first question, then address the second question. Both activities would start with risk assessment team setting a plan of action for approval by the risk manager and stakeholder group, then carrying out the plan. The plan of action would include assessment and measurement endpoints, budget, deliverables, schedules, etc. The team set up a plan of action, including what data would be sought and from where, what would be done with the data, what information would be obtained, and how it would be presented to the risk manager for the decision stage. This plan was presented back to the risk manager, approved, and followed. Results of the risk assessment were presented to the risk manager, who consulted with the stakeholders.

The second iteration of the assessment examined the question of ecosystem harm, which led to careful and detailed deliberation within the risk assessment team. The risk assessment team knew that the risk manager could not possibly want a full ecological assessment, and proposed some options to the risk manager. Questions, plans, and options presented were based on prior experience and knowledge of this type of activity. These questions led to discussion of the availability of relevant data. Subsequently, the ecological modelers were consulted regarding the utility of the available data. The risk assessment team then worked with the risk manager to finalize the detailed questions, determine the assessment and measurement endpoints, and complete a conceptual model for the assessment. The problem formulation included the designing of an action plan or work plan, including experiments, measurements, and endpoints.

Recommendations for unresolved technical issues and system requirements

The following recommendations were made:

1) The case replicate group encountered only routine technical problems that had been identified earlier in the conference. These were availability (existence) of site-specific data on chemicals, animal species, and temporal trends.

2) This case identified a need for databases detailing local, state, and federal laws and regulations. The decision-support system needs access to some kind of stakeholder database that identifies groups and/or individuals that should be consulted, and perhaps details how that consultation should occur. In conducting this case study example, the scientists had a tendency to jump past the stakeholder involvement, assuming that the risk manager had taken care of that step.

3) There is a need for experimental design and management tools (schedule, budget, etc.) to assist in the problem-formulation stage.

4) We need a structured process to prevent the experts from jumping ahead in defining the problem and in performing the remaining components of the assessment.

5) The decision-support system should provide for convenient and systematic documentation of the assumptions, implicit and explicit, involved in the assessment.

Case study III - spotted owl

Introduction and objectives

Following the role-playing and review of the case studies, participants from different component groups were asked to consider the risk-assessment system from the perspective of the spotted owl case study. This discussion focused on review of each of the component groups and how the components could or would be handled in the context of the spotted owl case study. This exercise was not a comprehensive assessment of the system with respect to the spotted owl. Rather, it primarily sought to identify whether the system could reasonably capture the process of risk assessment for this problem (Figure B-4).

The participants sought to answer a series of 6 questions revolving around the spotted

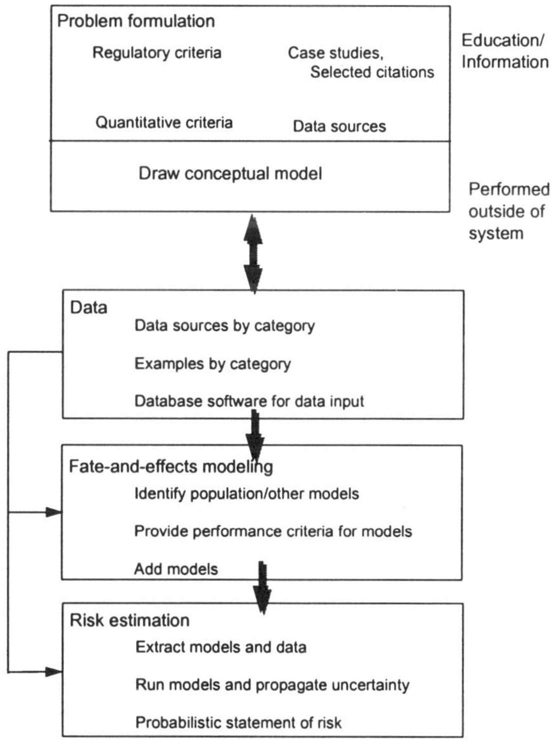

Figure B-4 Prototype for spotted owl ecological risk assessment

owl decision specifically and natural resource issues in general. First, it was determined that a risk assessment could be accomplished, even one that had objectives broader than the one discussed in the role-playing session; specifically, will Option 9, the recommended option, protect the spotted owl? Option 9 allows thinning of plantations up to 80 years of age, salvage of dead trees, and extra protection for at-risk species. It was determined that the question was expandable to incorporate economic information into the risk management scheme. This expansion would allow us to make an assessment of the range of management options proposed to ensure the survival of the spotted owl. However, this case study addressed only Option 9.

After deciding that the risk assessment was possible, the question was posed whether or not some support system would be of use in making the risk assessment. The group decided that such a system would be useful. It then identified how that system would be beneficial and who would be able to benefit from its use (see Table B-2).

Table B-2   Issues and users that would benefit from a support system

Issue	User
Identify available models and data	Risk assessor
Identify regulatory requirements and critical criteria (e.g., extinction thresholds)	Risk manager, assessor
Determine the feasibility of performing the risk assessment	Risk manager
Use as a educational tool to learn about the process and components of risk assessment	Risk manager, public
Standardize assessment methods, inclusion of uncertainty, and publication of results	Risk manager, public
Prioritize research issues by evaluating gaps and areas of greatest uncertainty in models and data	Risk manager, assessor, public

These issues became the objectives for the proposed support system. After determining how the various information and computational elements from the risk assessment process were conducted for the spotted owl case study, the group returned to the objectives to determine if the objectives were met.

The group decided that the ERADSS should function in the problem-formulation phase only as an information provider. We did not envision the system providing assessment endpoints as an output, nor did we see the system as forcing the user through a rigid series of decisions. Information viewed as useful in this context included: regulatory information (e.g., Endangered Species Act, Migratory Bird Treaty); indexes to scientific data and information that could be used to determine criteria such as extinction probabilities; and citations for similar problems and solutions. In addition, the system was viewed as a potential source to locate any data concerning past or present abundances of spotted owls and other data relating to land cover and habitat characteristics of affected areas in the Northwest. These data would be used by the risk assessor and risk manager to develop the conceptual model and identify assessment and measurement endpoints. However, development of the conceptual model and endpoint identification would be performed by the analysis and risk manager outside of the support system.

During the fate-and-effects segment of the analysis, the system provides a list of models (e.g., habitat relations, population, timber harvest) that might be applicable to this problem. Models would be listed along with their performance criteria for various classes of users. Models would not be contained within the system. The risk estimate segment of the system would provide a computational platform in which the models could be brought into the system and combined in any necessary manner. The system would help bring the data into the system, either from an established database or from direct input to the analysis. These data would be linked to the appropriate models and the models run to provide estimates of exposure and effects. The results could be combined in the risk-estimation phase of the analysis. Uncertainties would be propagated through the models and the risk estimate developed.

Glossary

adverse effects:
> A deleterious effect in an individual or higher level of biological organization which results in impairment of functional capacity or capacity to compensate for additional stress or increased susceptibility to other environmental influences. (van Leeuwen 1995)

assessment endpoint:
> An explicit expression of the environmental value that is to be protected. (USEPA 1992)

biological scale:
> Dimensions in space and time that are characteristic and relevant to the life history, behavior, growth, and reproduction of organisms. The juxtaposition of biological scales with the scales of exposure is important in assessing ecological risk.

characterization of uncertainty (uncertainty characterization or analysis):
> Process that assesses the imperfect knowledge concerning the present or future state of the system under study; may be qualitative and/or quantitatively addressed.

conceptual model:
> The conceptual model describes a series of working hypotheses of how the stressor might affect ecological components. The conceptual model also describes the ecosystem potentially at risk, the relationship between measurement and assessment endpoints, and exposure scenarios. (USEPA 1992)

deterministic analysis:
> An analysis in which all population and environmental parameters are assumed to be constant and accurately specified. (Suter 1993)

ecological receptor:
> The ecological entity exposed to the stressor. Ecological entity refers to a species, group of species, an ecosystem function or characteristic, or a specific habitat. (USEPA 1996)

ecological risk assessment decision-support system (ERADSS):
> A computer-based system that facilitates the conduct of an ecological risk assessment, complete with data sources, assumptions, models, and other tools in order to enable harmonized risk assessment-based decision-making.

ecological scale:
> Dimensions in time and space that are characteristic and relevant to the structure and function of populations, communities, and ecosystems. The

juxtaposition of ecological scales with the scales of exposure is important in assessing ecological risk.

ecosystem:

The biotic community and abiotic environment within a specified location in space and time. (USEPA 1992)

environmental risk management:

The process of evaluating alternative actions and selecting among them. Environmental risk management is a decision-making process that entails consideration of political, social, economic, and engineering information with environmental risk-related information to develop, analyze, and compare options and to select the appropriate response to a potential environmental risk. The selection process requires the use of value judgments on such issues as the acceptability of the environmental risk and the reasonableness of the costs of control. (adapted from National Research Council 1983)

expected loss:

The product of risk and the magnitude of the adverse event.

expert systems:

A logical problem-solving process (often computerized) that steps the user through a series of questions based on a documented decision-making process. Such a system could include artificial intelligence aspects and could coordinate models, data, interpretation and presentation of results in a highly interactive user interface. (Bartell et al. 1992)

geographic information system (GIS):

A computerized integration of database management system technology with automated mapping to capture, store, retrieve, display, analyze, and relate information graphically in order to facilitate its use and interpretation spatially. (Douglas 1995)

geographic scale:

The spatial extent of ecosystem exposure.

Latin hypercube sampling:

Stratified random sampling used to select one set of values of the effects factors from a representative distribution during a simulation. This procedure divides each parameter distribution into an equal probability regions where n is the number of simulations. (Bartell et al. 1992)

measurement endpoint:

A measurable ecological characteristic that is related to the valued characteristic chosen as the assessment endpoint. Measurement endpoints are often expressed as the statistical or arithmetic summaries of the observations that comprise the measurement. (USEPA 1992)

Monte Carlo simulation:

> A technique used to obtain information about the propagation of uncertainty in mathematical simulation models. It is an iterative process involving the random selection of model parameter values from specified frequency distributions, simulation of the system, and output of predicted values. The distribution of the output values can be used to determine the probability of occurrence of any particular value given the uncertainty in the parameters. (Suter 1993)

probabilistic analysis:

> An assessment in which effects, exposure, and environmental parameters are represented by statistical distributions (e.g., results of such an assessment might be a 90% probability of having a 50% reduction in a fish population); non-distributional approaches may also be used.

problem formulation:

> First phase of an ecological risk assessment that establishes the goals, breadth and focus of the assessment. It is a systematic planning step that identifies the major factors to be considered, linked to the regulatory and policy context of the assessment. (USEPA 1992)

quantitative structure-activity relationships (QSARs):

> The relationship between the physical and/or chemical properties of substances and their ability to cause an effect, partition in the environment, enter into certain reactions, etc. (modified from van Leeuwen 1995)

risk characterization:

> A phase of ecological risk assessment that integrates the results of the exposure and ecological effects analyses to evaluate the likelihood of adverse ecological effects associated with exposure to a stressor. The ecological significance of the adverse effects is discussed, including consideration of the types of magnitudes of the effects, their spatial and temporal patterns, and the likelihood of recovery. (USEPA 1992)

risk management:

> The process of evaluating alternative actions and selecting among them. Risk management is a decision-making process that entails consideration of political, social, economic, and engineering information with risk-related information to develop, analyze, and compare options and to select the appropriate response to a potential risk. The selection process requires the use of value judgments on such issues as the acceptability of the risk and the reasonableness of the costs of control. (adapted from National Research Council 1983)

risk:

> The probability of a prescribed undesired effect. If the level of effect is treated

as an integer variable, risk is the product of the probability and frequency of effect [e.g., (probability of an accident) x (the number of expected mortalities)]. Risks result from the existence of hazard and uncertainty about its expression. (Suter 1993)

sensitivity analysis:
> The response of the state variables or model variables to changes in input parameters, functions, or submodels (adapted from Rand 1995)

stressor:
> Any physical, chemical, or biological entity that can induce an adverse response. (USEPA 1992)

temporal scale:
> The relevant time period for characterizing the nature (e.g., frequency, duration, timing) of the stressor and the ecological response.

uncertainty:
> Imperfect knowledge concerning the present or future state of the system under consideration; a component of risk resulting from imperfect knowledge of the degree of hazard or of its spatial and temporal pattern of expression. (Suter 1993)

References

Barnthouse LW. 1992. The role of models in ecological risk assessment. *Environ Toxicol Chem* 11:1751–1760.

Barnthouse LW. 1993. Population-level effects. In: Suter GW II, editor. Ecological risk assessment. Chelsea MI: Lewis Publishers. p 247–274.

Bartell SM, Gardner RH, O'Neill RV. 1992. Ecological risk estimation. Chelsea MI: Lewis Publishers. 252 p.

Bradbury SP, Henry TR, Niemi GJ, Carlson RW, Snarski VM. 1989. Use of respiratory-cardiovascular responses of rainbow trout (*Salmo gairdneri*) in identifying acute toxicity syndromes in fish. Part 3. Polar narcotics. *Environ Toxicol Chem* 8:247–261.

Burgman MA, Ferson S, Akcakaya HR. 1993. Risk assessment in conservation biology. ECOMED: Chapman and Hall. Population and Community Biology Series.

Burns LA. 1983. Validation of exposure models: the role of conceptual verification, sensitivity analysis, and alternative hypotheses. In: Bishop WE, Cardwell RD, Heidolph BB, editors. Aquatic toxicology and hazard assessment: 6th symposium. ASTM STP 802. Philadelphia PA: American Society for Testing and Materials. p 255–281.

Burns LA. 1986. Validation and verification of aquatic fate models. In: Environmental modelling for priority setting among existing chemicals. Workshop proceedings. Landsberg, Munich, Germany: Ecomed. p 148–172.

Cardwell RD, Parkhurst BR, Warren-Hicks W, Volosin JS. 1993. Aquatic ecological risk. *Water Environ Tech* 5:47–51.

DeAngelis DL, Gross LJ, editors. 1992. Individual-based models and approaches in ecology. New York: Chapman and Hall. 544 p.

Douglas WJ. 1995. Environmental GIS. Applications to industrial facilities. Boca Raton FL: Lewis.

[EC] European Commission. 1994. Guidance on risk assessment for new and existing substances. Brussels, Belgium: Luxemborg Office for Official Publications of the European Communities.

Faber M, Manstetten R, Proops J. 1992. Toward an open future: ignorance, novelty and evolution. In: Constanza R, Norton BG, Haskell BD, editors. Ecosystem health: new goals for environmental management. Washington DC: Island Pr.

Fava JA, Adams WJ, Larson RJ, Dickson GW, Dickson KL, Bishop WE, eidtors. 1987. Research priorities in environmental risk assessment. Pensacola FL: SETAC.

Ferson S. 1994. Naive Monte Carlo methods yield dangerous underestimates of tail probabilities. Proceedings of the high consequence safety symposium. Albuquerque NM: Sandia National Laboratories.

Ferson S, Kuhn R. 1992. Propagating uncertainty in ecological risk analysis using interval and fuzzy arithmetic. In: Zannetti P, editor. Computer techniques in environmental studies IV. London: Elsevier Applied Science. p 387–401

Ferson S, Long TF. 1994. Conservative uncertainty propagation in environmental risk assessments. In: Hughes JS, Biddinger GR, Mones E, editors. Environmental toxicology and risk assessment, vol. 3. ASTM STP 1218. Philadelphia PA: ASTM. 413 p.

Finkel A. 1990. Confronting uncertainty in risk management. Washington DC: Center for Risk Management, Resources for the Future.

Ginzburg LR, Slobokin LB, Johnson K, Bindman AG. 1982. Quasiextinction probabilities as a measure of impact on population growth. *Risk Anal* 2(3):171–181.

Glaz J, Johnson BMK. 1984. Probability inequalities for multivariate distributions with dependence structures. *J Am Statistical Assoc* 79:436–440.

Health Council of the Netherlands. 1993. Ecotoxicological risk assessment and policy-making in the Netherlands—dealing with uncertainties. *Network* 6(3)/7(1):8–11.

Iman RL, Conover WJ. 1980. Small sample sensitivity analysis techniques for computer models, with an application to risk assessment. *Communications in Statistics* A9:1749–1842.

Kaufman A, Gupta MM. 1985. Introduction to fuzzy arithmetic: theory and applications. New York: Van Nostrand Reinhold.

Mackay D, Paterson S. 1982. Fugacity revisited. *Environmental Science and Technology* 15:654A–660A.

Moore DRJ, Biddinger GR. 1995. The interaction between risk assessors and risk managers during the problem formulation stage. *Environ Toxicol Chem* 14(12):2013–2014.

[NOAA]. National Oceanic and Atmospheric Administration. 1993. Weather summaries. Asheville DC: National Climatic Data Center, Climate Services Division.

[NRC]. National Research Council. 1983. Risk assessment in the federal goverment: managing the process. Prepared by the National Research Council Committee on the institutional means for assessment of risks to public health. Washington DC: National Academy.

[NRC]. National Research Council. 1986. Ecological knowledge and problem-solving: concepts and case studies. Prepared by the National Research Council Committee on the application of ecological theory to environmental problems. Washington DC: National Academy. 388 p.

Rand, GM. 1995. Fundamentals of aquatic toxicology. Effects, environmental fate and risk assessment. 2nd ed. Washington DC: Taylor and Francis.

Rodier DJ, Mauriello DA. 1993. The quotient method for ecological risk assessment and modeling under TOSCA: A Review. In: Landis WG, Hughes JS, Lewis MA, editors. Environmental toxicology and risk assessment, ASTM 1179.

Russom CL, Anderson EB, Greenwood BE, Pilli A. 1991. ASTER: an integration of the AQUIRE database and the QSAR system for use in ecological risk assessments. In: Hermens JLM, Opperhuizen A, editors. QSAR in environmental toxicology-IV. Amsterdam NL: Elsevier p 667–670.

[STATSGO] State Soil Geographic Database. 1993. National Cartographic and Geographic Information Systems Center, USDA, Soil Conservation Service, Fort Worth TX.

Stewart-Oaten A. 1986. The before-after/control-impact pairs design for environmental impact. Prepared for Marine Review Committee, Inc., 531 Encinitas Blvd., Encinitas, CA 92024.

Suter GW. 1993. Ecological risk assessment. Ann Arbor MI: Lewis Publishers. 538 p.

Thomann RV. 1989. Bioaccumulation model of organic chemical distribution in aquatic food chains. *Environ Sci Technol* 23:699–707.

[USDOE] U.S. Department of Energy. 1994. Screening benchmarks for ecological risk assessment. draft report. Environmental Sciences Division. Oak Ridge TN: Oak Ridge National Laboratory.

[USEPA] U.S. Environmental Protection Agency. 1992. Framework for ecological risk assessment. EPA/630/R-92/001, Washington DC: USEPA, Office of Research and Development. p 41.

[USEPA] U.S. Environmental Protection Agency. 1993. A review of ecological assessment case studies from a risk assessment perspective. Volume II. EPA/630/R-92/005. Washington DC: USEPA, Office of Research and Development.

[USEPA] U.S. Environmental Protection Agency. 1994. A review of ecological assessment case studies from a risk assessment perspective. EPA/630/R-94/003. Washington DC: USEPA, Office of Research and Development.

[USEPA] U.S. Environmental Protection Agency. 1996. Proposed guidelines for ecological risk assessment . EPA/630/R-95/002B USEPA, Risk assessment forum, Washington DC: USEPA.

[USGS] U.S. Geological Survey. 1986. Land use and land cover digital data from 1:250,000 and 1:100,000 scale maps. Data user's guide 4. Reston VA: Earth Science Information Center.

[USGS] U.S. Geological Survey. 1993a. Manual of federal geographic data products. Federal geographic data committee. Reston VA: Earth Science Information Center.

[USGS] U.S. Geological Survey. 1993b. Digital elevation models. Reston VA: Earth Science Information Center.

[USGS] U.S. Geological Survey. 1993c. Hydrologic unit maps. Reston VA: Earth Science Information Center.

[USGS] U.S. Geological Survey. 1993d. National water summary. Reston VA: Earth Science Information Center.

van Leeuwen CJ. 1995. General Introduction In: van Leeuwen CJ, Hermens JH, editors. Risk assessment of chemicals: an introduction. Dordrecht, The Netherlands: Kluwer Academic Press.

Venkatram A. 1982. A framework for evaluating air quality models. *Boundary-Layer Meteorology* 24:371–385.

Venkatram A. 1983. Uncertainty in predictions from air quality models. *Boundary-Layer Meteorology* 27:185–196.

Wilson R, Crouch EAC. 1987. Risk assessment and comparisons: an introduction. *Science* 236:267–270.

Index